COVERING WOODEN BOATS
with FIBERGLASS

COVERING WOODEN BOATS
with FIBERGLASS

ALLAN H. VAITSES

INTERNATIONAL MARINE PUBLISHING COMPANY
Camden, Maine

Copyright © 1981, 1989 International Marine
Publishing Company

2 hardbound printings
First published in paperback 1989

10   9   8   7   6   5   4   3   2   1

Library of Congress Cataloging-in-Publication Data

Vaitses, Allan H.
     Covering wooden boats with fiberglass /
     Allan H. Vaitses.—Rev.
         p.   cm.
     ISBN 0-87742-997-9
     1. Fiberglass boats.   2. Wooden boats—Maintenance
and repair.
     I. Title.
     VM322.V34   1989
     623.8'207—dc20   89-20018
                                                                CIP

International Marine Publishing Company offers software
for sale. For information and a catalog, please contact TAB
Software Department, Blue Ridge Summit, PA 17294-0850.

Questions regarding the content of this book should be
addressed to:

International Marine Publishing Company
Division of TAB Books, Inc.
P.O. Box 220
Camden, ME 04843

Contents

Preface

To develop a process of sound fiberglass technique requires people with in-depth experience in the work. I was fortunate to have both Frank (Whitey) Mickivicki and John Andrews contributing their combined 60 years of knowledge to remind me of the dos and don'ts of fiberglass.

It was my long ambition to retire from boatbuilding to write, but writing this book before I retired was necessary if I were to do so without leaving business unfinished. Not many days passed in the last few years without an inquiry about covering a boat with fiberglass. Not that many of these callers were hot prospects for a small New England boat shop. What could the business do for a man across the country (or in another country) whose boat needed covering? To explain the process in some detail seemed mandatory if I knew what he should do, and if I also knew the mess he might get into if I didn't offer some guidelines. But the drain on my time was heavy and the amount of help possible by phone or letter too limited. While all this public education was perhaps an unavoidable part of being in the business, it left unanswered the question of what would happen when I retired. I hope this book is the answer to that question.

Introduction

About 25 years ago, I began developing a system for covering wooden boats with fiberglass that would not come off the boat — as most systems eventually *have* done. It's been an enlightening experience, as the case histories in Chapter 11 will show. As a result of this, I would like to say to anyone wondering whether or not to cover a wooden boat with fiberglass that yes, a fiberglass covering on your boat is as practical and seaworthy an exterior as any — if done correctly. Veteran boatbuilders are familiar with coverings that have failed in some way, so most of them believe it will not work. It doesn't matter whether the covering was done when the boat was manufactured or when she reached an advanced age; most of the usual fiberglass coverings have cracked or peeled off.

We once re-fiberglassed the bottom of a Rybovich sportfisherman that had been covered with two layers of glass cloth in epoxy resin, supposedly about 12 years before. It was a good job of its type to have lasted so long, but one day half of the bottom covering on one side fell off. Obviously, the epoxy had had a good grip on the planking, since almost every square inch of the fiberglass took some of the mahogany with it. A grainy, chunky veneer came away, leaving the boat's bottom striated and pitted, as though she had been dragged over a bed of spikes a hundred yards long. That the epoxy never did let go of the wood indicates an excellent bond: it is important to an understanding of fiberglass covering to note that it was not the glue but the wood that came apart.

More than 20 years ago, I had unwittingly predicted the eventual demise of this covering job. In an article submitted to *Yachting* magazine, I had stated that sticking fiberglass to wood is an "iffy" thing: it is usually successful on softwoods in a dry environment, less so on the harder woods, and bound to fail on a hardwood subjected to both bone dryness and complete saturation. I further stated that if one could weld steel plate to the surface of a hardwood as tightly as one can weld steel to steel, then the wood, when subjected to dry-to-saturated cycles, would simply shear itself apart close to the welded interface.

The editor rejected my article, and by way of explanation he sent along the comments of an executive of Owens-Corning's Fiberglas Division to whom he had sent it for appraisal. In essence, the comments were that I was wrong, that fiberglass could indeed be applied to any wood quite successfully as long as the work was "properly done" — the wood dry and sanded clean and the right materials and techniques used to cover it. Well how about that! I wondered what a boatbuilder-writer who has seen the failure of all kinds of "properly done" covering jobs should do.

Not anxious to attempt the re-education of these two gentlemen, I put the article aside. My time would be better spent on more amenable problems, including that of a reliable fiberglass covering for wooden boats. Such was not forthcoming overnight. Over the next several years in my custom boat shop, as covering jobs came in, I studied each with an eye to making it as indestructible as possible. Because my men and I were building tooling and prototypes for fiberglass boatbuilders and one-off boats in fiberglass as well as wood, we had no fear or mistrust of fiberglass. We had come to accept its many good qualities as natural complements to the wood with which we had already built more than a hundred boats. As the mother of a large family once told me, "There's always room in your heart for one more." That's equally true with any material or technique that contributes to the success of boatbuilding, especially if that's where your interests lie.

Anyway, during these years we learned to use more layers of glass and to apply the thickest practicable covering over the wood. We learned to use chopped strand matt because of its superior adhesion, resistance to peeling, and watertight integrity. We learned not to use the glass cloth that had long been considered the standard material for covering wood. Above all, we learned *always* to fasten the glass mechanically to the wood.

The sum of what we learned in that period is a covering system of fiberglass over wood that is thick enough to withstand both abuse on the outside and movement of the wood beneath, one that is watertight, and one that does not depend on chemical adhesion to the wood to remain fastened securely to the boat. In 25 years, no job that has been done with strict adherence to the precepts of this system has failed.

It seems reasonable, because of the lack of deterioration apparent in these jobs, that this system may share the indefinite life expectancy that both fiberglass and wood have when used properly and individually. The growing fleet of boats enjoying good health under a sturdy skin of fiberglass ranges from 12 to 65 feet: high-speed powerboats, power cruisers, lobster boats, heavy fishing boats, and sailboats (from small, open centerboarders to deep-keel auxiliaries). Some were covered while being built, some when 60 years old, some while in an extremely robust condition, and one while in such critical condition that she had to be covered where she was, because haulers refused to transport her. Other boats hovered on the brink of oblivion for want of extensive rebuilding, until we covered them with enough fiberglass to refit them for a second life afloat.

They number nearly 50 boats that my firm had a hand in, a couple of hundred that we know were covered by several North American companies that took up the work, and an untallied number covered by others following our advice and/or example. Fishing every day, or yachting every season, each of these jobs, done our way, has piled up proof that covering wooden boats with fiberglass will work. Not only can you make the fiberglass stay on, you can make a boat stay together with it, too.

1/ Why Do It?

FOR WATERTIGHT INTEGRITY

From its earliest days, fiberglass has been used to cover wooden decks and trunk tops. (The term "fiberglass" is a shortened version of "glass fiber reinforced plastic.") Fiberglass is tougher, easier to apply, and much easier to maintain and repair than canvas. Even a single layer of glass cloth, which makes the worst possible fiberglass covering job, has about the same life expectancy as canvas. This easily attained superiority over previous covering materials probably accounts for the fact that, to date, few of the thousands of fiberglass coverings on wooden decks have been anywhere near as watertight or as durable as they could have been. (But more about that later.) There has been a general failure to realize the full potential of fiberglass, though it seems to be accepted that fiberglass can make a wooden deck watertight.

When it comes to hulls, some of the earliest applications of fiberglass were precipitated by the urgent need to restore watertight integrity to older boats. This indicates, again, the widespread recognition of the material's potential for sealing out water. Of course, fiberglass also has long been applied to canoes and other small boats that formerly might have had a canvas outer skin. (In those instances, due to the thin, softwood planking, the fiberglass has usually hung on very nicely.) And it didn't take builders long to discover that the application of fiberglass to a new plywood boat had a fair chance of success. But doubts have been raised by the eventual physical failure of many coverings. That these were usually due to the almost universal use of a thin, glass cloth covering — a covering that was always ready to let the water through after minimal impact, abrasion, or "working" of the wood — is an important lesson that those early failures (and some that are still happening) have taught us. The other side of the coin is that, even when the reinforcement is only cloth, fiberglass can seal out water for some time.

What this book will show you is how to seal out water completely and indefinitely.

FOR LESS MAINTENANCE

Impervious to weather for years without refinishing, and for decades without deterioration of its physical properties, fiberglass is unquestionably the most carefree of the common hull materials. Nor do the surfaces of wooden boats covered with appropriate thicknesses of fiberglass demand any more maintenance than those of solid fiberglass boats. This does not mean that the two surfaces — a fiberglass covering or solid fiberglass — are equally slick at their beginnings, or even that the materials are exactly the same, although they certainly can be. It means only that whatever the condition of your boat originally, the maintenance needs of the fiberglass, whether over a wooden boat or free standing, will be the same. Naturally, that statement only applies with certainty to fiberglass coverings that are more

Finish work underway on the fiberglass-covered Wianno Senior Mimi, *which was built in 1917 by Crosby of Osterville, Massachusetts.*

substantial than the ubiquitous one- or two-layer glass cloth jobs. But one thing we don't have to qualify is the vast superiority, as to care, of fiberglass over the relatively vulnerable and unstable surface of wood. Fiberglass will not rot, it has no grain to be raised or split by weathering, and it has no seams that will open and crack paint when dry or close and extrude compound when water-soaked.

FOR PHYSICAL STRENGTH

The amount of glass in a laminate is the true measure of its strength. Even the too-thin fiberglass coverings so common in the past add considerable "hoop strength" to a boat, at least until it is burst by the restless wood. But since a properly thick laminate of fiberglass by itself can make as strong a boat as any, it is only logical that the thicker the covering, the more strength it will add to a boat: right up to the extreme where the strength of the wooden boat becomes inconsequential. At some point, the laminate's strength will surpass that of the wood.

The author's son, Steve, on board his fiberglass-covered Crane sloop, Katama. She was built in 1914 and covered when she neared the age of 60.

Then if the wood should want to move, it might break its bond to the fiberglass, but it would not crack what is essentially a fiberglass hull around it.

We have put that much fiberglass on some wooden hulls that had lost their ability to carry on. It works out well to have a new fiberglass hull around a fine, old wooden boat. On the first few such boats, we used every bit as much fiberglass as the same size solid fiberglass hull would have, and perhaps a little bit more. After all, we had had no previous experience to indicate what would happen. But as time went on, we began to realize that, no matter how weakened she was as a structure, all those strakes of planking, backbone members, frames, deck beams, decking, and bulkheads were reinforcing our fiberglass more heavily and continuously than any all-fiberglass boat is strengthened by whatever core or stiffeners she might have.

Yet the parts of a wooden boat only strengthen a

A plywood Dutch Treat being moved out of the shop after her hull was covered.

covering as long as they are well fastened to it. Therefore, we soon began to place more emphasis on fastening the glass and wood together mechanically, cutting back the amount of fiberglass enough to allow for the considerable strength and stiffness remaining in the wooden structure. This philosophy has meant that we have used less glass in all coverings — never so little, however, on the soundest boats that the wood would be likely to overpower the laminate, never so little that the laminate could be punctured easily by ordinary impacts, never with just glass cloth, and *never* without those mechanical fastenings.

There can be no doubt that enough glass can restore the physical strength of any wooden boat worth saving. Sometimes it doesn't take as much as one might think, and sometimes it takes an awful lot in certain crucial spots. It may be necessary, or at least less expensive, to add some new, sound wood to the old structure before covering it. However challenging and gratifying it may be to bring a good, old boat back from the shadow of death, there is even greater satisfaction in catching a boat in declining health and rejuvenating her with a tough, new fiberglass hide. Better still is a new wooden boat with a proper fiberglass covering. A wooden boat like that has the best of both worlds, and it's a boat to go outdoors with, too.

2/ Rot, Weight, and Cost

One of the first questions people ask about covering a wooden boat with fiberglass is, "Will it make her rot?"

Rot in a boat is always attended by a certain degree of dampness. It's not wood underwater or fully saturated wood that rots; neither is it tinder-dry wood. Rather, rot only seems to take hold in wood that has been kept damp by a trickle of water (usually from a leak) or from condensation in a poorly ventilated place. Rot also seems to require some air or oxygen as well as moderate temperatures.

It has always been our opinion that favorable conditions for rot cannot exist at the interface of watertight, unbroken fiberglass-and-wood. We have never heard of a case where it did. Of course, one might find rotting wood below a ruptured fiberglass deck covering, just as one might find it below a leak in any wooden deck. My point is simply that neither dampness nor air is likely to exist in favorable amounts for rot at the interface of a covering as long as the covering remains tight.

As to the surface of the wood on the interior of the boat, it will be kept rot-free by proper ventilation, which is about all that is needed to supplement the absence of leaks. Not that a generous application of copper naphthanate or other wood preservative from time to time isn't good insurance. It's just that ventilation should always be available.

But if the proof of the pudding is in the eating, it must be reiterated that there are both new and very old boats that we covered 20 or so years ago with no rot yet reported. In view of this fact, coupled with the well-documented nature of rot, the indications are that a watertight fiberglass covering outside and good ventilation inside create conditions that are about as unfavorable for rot as one could ask for.

Another frequent question about fiberglass covering is, "How much weight does it add to a boat?"

That's easy to figure. A square foot of fiberglass ⅛ inch thick in all, with a proper glass/resin ratio, weighs one pound. If a boat has 500 square feet of hull surface, a covering ⅛ inch thick will weigh 500 pounds, and a covering ¼ inch thick will weigh 1,000 pounds. Now, although boats come in all sorts of proportions of length, beam, and draft — so that a 25-foot-overall cat-boat with 12-foot beam and a 32-foot Novi lobster boat with 10-foot beam might have about the same total surface area — the construction of a wooden boat with 500 square feet of hull surface will probably be such that a ⅛-inch-thick laminate will do an excellent job if the hull is sound. If the garboard planks are sprung, or if the fastenings in the bottom are in poor condition, or if the entire hull is decrepit, then it is necessary to apply additional layers over the problem areas. However, a boat this size will rarely be so feeble as to need more than an average laminate thickness of ¼ inch, or 1,000 pounds, of fiberglass.

Suppose we decide to put 700 pounds of fiberglass on this particular hull. She will weigh 700 pounds more than she did before, but she will not settle as much in the water as she would if the entire 700 pounds were taken aboard. The part of the fiberglass that is underwater displaces water, having made the boat bigger by its volume. If, for instance, 450 of the 700 pounds are underwater, about 300 pounds of that 450 will be treading water. Therefore, only the remaining 150 underwater pounds, plus the 300 pounds that are above the water — a total of 450 pounds — will be working to settle the boat lower in the water. (See Appendix for more details.)

For those interested in calculating the effect of a particular laminate on a given boat: fiberglass weighs 95 pounds per cubic foot, salt water weighs 64 pounds per cubic foot, and fresh water is 62 pounds per cubic foot. This is easy to remember when it is reduced to the simple rule that about two-thirds of the weight of immersed fiberglass is supported by the water it displaces.

Getting back to a hypothetical boat with 500 square feet of hull surface, only the high performance of a light-displacement boat in this size range would be affected noticeably by 700 pounds of added total displacement. Nor would 450 pounds of negative buoyancy increase the draft of most hull shapes with this area as much as an inch. But there is another effect of covering a wooden boat that sometimes cancels out all or most of the added weight.

Wood immersed in water soaks up huge amounts of it as time goes by, and the underwater part of a boat gets heavier and heavier during its weeks, months, or years afloat. The magnitude of this gain in weight is well known to those of us who have lifted a small boat around easily after dry storage but could hardly budge her after a season in the water. A good fiberglass covering can seal out that water and will keep the boat's weight more or less constant (although admittedly greater by the weight of the laminate). Some boats that we have covered with heavy thicknesses of fiberglass actually floated higher afterward, because their wood had been so waterlogged from living in the water year in and year out. Often, boats that normally spend only a few months of the year in the water have been found to float on about the same waterline after covering as they would have at the end of a season without it. This is especially true if a boat has been leaking and saturating the interior as well as the exterior. At first, we used to raise the waterline after covering any boat. Now we only bother to do that on a boat that has been floating too close to the line anyway.

Naturally, the soakage factor depends on the type of construction. Soakage is usually slight or nonexistent on a cold-molded or laminated hull, or a deck with good glue barriers; it can be tremendous, however, in a construction using a great deal of heavy natural lumber with a more or less porous traditional paint job. But, though individual cases vary, it is safe to say that the weight of a substantial fiberglass covering does little or no harm to the vast majority of wooden boats.

The most frequently asked question about covering wooden boats with fiberglass is: "What would it cost?"

Just so I don't mislead anyone, I should say that to do it right won't be cheap. In 1989, the mixture of fiberglass materials needed ranged from $1.50 to $2.00 per pound at wholesale prices. (See Appendix.) The cost of materials can be predicted quite accurately by multiplying the number of square feet to be covered by the number of ⅛-inch-thick increments in the thickness desired. This total number of ⅛-inch-thick square feet is the number of pounds needed, and (currently) half of the number of wholesale dollars. (The quantities of specific materials involved in a given laminate will become apparent in Chapter 3.) The formula for total materials cost is:

$$\frac{\text{area x thickness}}{\frac{1}{8}''} = \text{total weight}$$

and total weight times price per lb. equals cost of materials.

When it comes to the amount of labor involved in

covering a given boat, it is difficult to be precise. The shape and details of the particular boat, the experience of those working on her, the working conditions, and the equipment available will all affect the total hours involved in covering her. Further, the cost of these hours is completely subjective, depending as it does on the value that the laborers place on their time.

For a ballpark guide, two experienced men will average about two days (that's four man-days) to put the four layers totaling ⅛ inch of fiberglass on one side of a hull that has about 250 square feet of surface per side. A third man will need about a half-day to go along fastening the first and second layers before the third and fourth are applied. He will need much longer than that if he doesn't have a power fastening tool.

For obvious reasons, the time it might take to remove the hardware and reinstall it over the fiberglass, to reinstall rails, or to cut a rabbet for the termination of the covering will vary with every boat.

On deck work, two men can put two layers on a very large, plain, easily reached area in a half-day. They can also spend more time than that putting the same two layers on a pair of complicated, small, narrow side decks where there are bulwarks or toe rails to be covered; or on a cockpit with seats, hatches, and coamings. But while it is difficult to generalize about the amount of labor to expect on deck work, the covering materials can be estimated just about as accurately as hull materials.

When it comes time to put a paint or gelcoat finish on the covering job, we find owners' attitudes toward surface finish too divergent to allow more than some basic hints at the man-hours of the cosmetic stage. Each application of putty and the subsequent power sanding of it can take from one to two man-days on 250 square feet of topsides — and two man-days on that much bottom if it is overhead work on a racing bottom. These figures should be at least tripled for each round of hand block sanding. It is a matter of conscientiousness (or vanity) that determines how many times to go around sanding and filling and whether to brush the paint or spray it. However, those who relish a slick finish should be generous in allocating time (which is, of course, one kind of money) to this phase of covering. Meanwhile, the outlay for materials with which to finish a covering job is about the same as would be required to put a good finish on any other type of surface, starting in the rough.

The good news about the finish on a covering job is that it is semipermanent, like the finish on all fiberglass boats, due to the stability of the underlying material. Whatever the cost of covering a given wooden boat, the job will pay big dividends over the years in maintenance costs alone. A few years' yard bills that would have been expected for refinishing a wooden surface will pay for most covering jobs. For those who maintain their own boats, it should not take too many years to amortize the cost of materials for a covering job, especially in terms of refinishing materials that will now be needed rarely. A covered boat's seams will never need recaulking, repaying, sanding down, or filling. Good paint work (or whatever finish is on the fiberglass) will not puff out, peel, or break up at every seam every year, as it is likely to do on older wooden boats.

The savings in refinishing costs will be added to future savings in forestalled structural repairs due to the conservation of physical strength by the covering. Fastenings no longer need to be replaced, bad seams no longer nag, keelbolts are no longer a worry, and cracked ribs are no longer under surveillance. Nor should we forget the least tangible but most important gain: renewed confidence and freedom from the shadow of calamities large and small, whether it be water suddenly rising over the cabin sole or just a berth made miserably wet with drips from the overhead.

The worse the condition of the boat before covering, the more extensive and expensive the repairs needed to the wood and the more money will be saved by covering her. When today's labor costs are taken into account, a boat does not have to be all that bad before the covering job is cheaper than repair.

All things considered, fiberglass covering is indisputably cost-effective. Having seen what it does for a boat, I wouldn't be without it on new boat or old. It simply takes too much patience, time, and money to maintain wood on a boat that is less protected, no matter how much one loves wood; and I, for one, have always been especially fond of the stuff in all its wonderful varieties.

Just one word of warning: although a substantial covering can without question rejuvenate the most moribund relic, you should ask yourself at least three times about such a job, "Why do it?" If a boat is an inferior model, lacking graceful lines, good performance, or pleasant accommodations, why indeed revive her? Not every old wooden boat is a classic. Plenty of dogs have been built in the past. If the wreck in hand has no outstanding worth that cries out for continued enjoyment, better consign it to duty as landfill and seek out one of the thousands of good, old boats out there that richly deserve reincarnation. Don't fall in love with the process — get a good boat out of it.

3/ Choosing Laminates and Fastenings

I once received a call from an insurance agent. He said he'd been trying to place some insurance on Mr. C's boat. The company didn't like the fact that she was 40 years old, so they were quoting an outrageous rate, subject to survey.

"Did you tell them that we just covered her with six to 10 layers of fiberglass?" I asked.

"I sure did. Know what the man said? 'That don't work.' "

So there you are. The insurer, like everyone who spends any time in boatyards, had seen the eruption of once-smooth decks and hulls that had been covered with glass cloth. He is convinced, "That don't work." As long as builders and repairers continue to use glass cloth coverings, there are going to be more failures, and more people saying, "That don't work."

Examine a piece of glass cloth closely, and you will see that it is constructed just like a strainer. It is a mass of holes neatly arranged by woven strands. Lay it up on your deck and you have a deck covered with a strainer that happens to be clogged with resin. Crack the resin, and any of these holes or rows of holes will crack right through, top to bottom. As far as water is concerned, a crack from top to bottom in any material is a place to seep through.

Examine a piece of chopped-strand matt and you will see that it is constructed of several layers of small strands running in random directions. You can find an occasional tiny hole through this matted tangle, but you'll never mistake it for cloth. The difference, then, is that resin-impregnated matt has no clear resin pools running from top to bottom of the layer. Every drop, you might say, has glass strands running through it in depth and in different directions. This is the best construction to resist water penetration and propagation of cracks from top to bottom of the layer.

Matt also resists peeling much better than cloth. Having no continuous strands, a piece will break out of the layer rather than continue to pull away the rest of the material. Cloth usually rips off in sheets once it is started.

I am not going to discuss the various flexible cloths and flexible resins that are said to be unshakable because they expand and contract with the surface of the wood as it shrinks and swells. Nor am I going to get into epoxy saturation of the wood, which petrifies the wood so that it cannot shrink or swell. I have used some of these processes and I agree with the philosophy behind them. But it remains to be seen whether they will be developed to a point where they yield the same amount of indefinitely durable physical strength, combined with watertight integrity, per dollar's worth of material and hour's worth of labor that we get with a proper, fastened-on polyester-and-glass laminate.

To outline the covering job in one sentence: you are going to lay up some layers of fiberglass on the hull, secure them all over with fastenings a few inches apart, and then lay up some more layers. This is the essence of the covering that we have found to work best. The details will vary from boat to boat, but the basic structure of the covering should not be altered. There should always be some fiberglass, many fastenings, and then more fiberglass.

The first segment of the laminate could be any number of layers of glass deemed appropriate for the particular boat. On a very small, thinly planked craft we might use one layer of chopped-strand matt fastened with light staples. On a heavy fishing vessel we would need a massive laminate of alternate layers of matt and roving through which to drive some equally stout fastenings. It's a matter of proportioning the laminate and its fastenings to the construction on which they have to remain. The hull is strengthened and contained by the laminate, while the inevitable movement of the wood is compensated for through a faint bending of the fastenings. (See Appendix for more details.)

I like soft matt best for covering all kinds of boats. It's fragile and has to be handled deftly, or everything from one's hands to the bottom of the resin pot will be a mass of fuzz. When you get used to it, though, you'll do better work, do it more quickly, and use less resin.

Now, before anyone becomes upset by the prospect of designing a different fastened-on portion of the laminate for each boat, let me say that we have worked out a basic minimum combination. One layer of 1½-ounce matt with one layer of 18-ounce roving over it works very well on yachts and lighter workboats over 20 feet and under 50 feet. We settled on this pair of layers because it has precisely the properties needed in the fastened-on portion, and no fat, thus minimizing cost. But we also use it because two layers give enough latitude in the hardening stage to allow complete fastening before the fiberglass becomes impenetrable without drilling. More layers not only take longer to lay up but give off more heat, which further shortens the span between the "green" stage and the hard stage.

We put the matt on first to seal the interface and to back up the roving. If roving were put on first, it would be subject to moisture from the wood or the seams. (Roving's continuous strands have been known to carry water by capillary action.) Also, the matt has superior adhesion — to the hull for the short term and to the roving forevermore. The roving is used for the enormous hoop strength of its continuous strands, which bind up the wooden hull like innumerable small steel bands. These strands, caught under the bar of a staple or the head of a nail or screw, become a web that holds the entire laminate fast to the hull.

The fastenings we have found most useful, for four reasons, are heavy staples: (1) the staple's bar is sure to clamp a good number of strands of fiberglass to the hull; (2) the bar will allow some tiny movement of the strands while the legs prevent their escape; (3) staples can be driven very quickly with an air-powered, automatic gun; and (4) staples are light and cheap enough to be used in great numbers for the closely spaced attachment that we consider all-important.

We prefer galvanized staples because they cling in the wood best, and we think they will last a long time when buried in the wood under a watertight laminate. Admittedly, bronze staples are better at corrosion resistance, and Monel are best. But both are much more expensive, and the bronze is both weaker and too easily pulled out. We also prefer divergent staples, those whose legs angle off in the wood due to asymmetrical sawtooth leading edges, which direct one leg ahead and the other back.

We have fastened fiberglass with shingle nails, ring nails, wood screws, and (into an iron keel or such) machine screws. We have even cartridge-fired hardened steel nails through the glass into a steel hull. In fact, almost any kind of fastenings can be used, as long as they pin the glass to the hull securely and are closely spaced.

There's one thing certain. Cured fiberglass is harder than a Pharaoh's heart, so if we don't catch the fastened-on layers at the half-hard stage, before the resin has fully set up, we'll be forced to drill through it for any ordinary, untempered fastenings. On the other hand, in some situations the only practical procedure is to let the resin harden and either drill into it or drive hardened fastenings. For instance, if a very heavy laminate is to be applied to a massive construction, it is only common sense to have the fastenings' heads locking on a thicker portion of the laminate. In this case we will undoubtedly have to drill for them, since about four layers are the most we can put on before the hardening process gets ahead of the fastening.

After fastening, we apply the outer portion of the laminate. On any boat over 20 feet long, this should not be fewer than two layers of 1½-ounce matt. Matt is the most watertight material, and two layers of this easiest-to-apply weight of it is the minimum amount to ensure a durable, impact-resistant, watertight seal. These two layers, then, added to the two fastened-on layers, make up the basic four-layer hull covering for boats in the 20-foot to 40-foot range. These figures do not contradict the earlier statement that the two fastened-on layers are basic up to 50 feet. When the boat is over 40 feet we often use an extra set of matt and roving (one layer of each) as our basic covering over the fastened-on set and under the final two layers of matt.

As long as the hull is structurally sound, the basic four-layer cover does a good job. On boats under 25 feet, this covering will also correct a considerable degree of weakness in the fastenings, planking, or ribs. But on any boat, because of the hazards of collision and grounding, the entire covering on one side should overlap the other around the stem and across the bottom of the keel. On the larger boats, or those with lead or iron ballast keels, additional U-shaped layers, their arms reaching well up the sides of the keel, should cap the doubled covering on the bottom.

22

An unsound hull, as we've said, will need more than the basic four layers to bring it back to complete soundness. That enough layers in the right places will do this with such ease is one of the strongest arguments for fiberglass covering. So if we are covering a boat that is generally sound except that her planking is working (a little loose and always cracking the paint and putty), then it might be wise to add two more layers to the basic four. In this case one layer of matt and one of roving should be put on over the fastened-on layers, before putting on the rest of the laminate.

If only the garboard planks have been difficult to keep tight, we would use two to four additional layers of alternate matt and roving in and around that area. If she is a powerboat and the keel is a bit wobbly, or a sailboat whose ballast keelbolts are suspect, we would decide on the number of extra layers, encase the errant keel with them, use bored-for fastenings on either side of the join we're worried about (through all but the two final sealing layers of matt), and then stop worrying.

Your covering should be constructed with a low- or no-wax resin to avoid bad secondary bonds. However, you should use wax in the final layers to allow complete hardening of the fiberglass; or you should put wax in a final glazing coat of resin, if you want to be able to sand it without gumming up the sandpaper. When a resin, gelcoat, or other resin-based product has wax in it, the wax floats to the surface and seals off the laminate from the air. Otherwise, air inhibits curing at the surface and causes surface tack. Without something to keep its surface air-free, resin may remain soft enough to gum up sandpaper for days, sometimes for months. The good part about wax, then, is that it produces a sandable surface. The bad part is that after 12 to 24 hours, you *must* sand the dry wax away if you want to apply anything else to that surface and get a good bond.

It is not necessary to switch to a different resin; you can buy the wax additive under assorted trade names like Additive 10 or Tack Free. You can also make your own by dissolving paraffin wax (shaved thin and heated to the melting point) in styrene monomer. You can buy the styrene at your resin supply house, and you can buy the wax in a supermarket or at some Gulf gasoline stations. (See Appendix for more details.)

If you mix your own additive, mix it with your wax-free resin at the rate of at least one gram of the wax itself (not counting the weight of the styrene it is dissolved in) per two quarts of resin. If you buy it, ask the supplier how much to add. If he doesn't know, just add a spoonful to a pot, try more or less in the next, and you'll soon know more than he did about it.

In Chapter 11 we will describe the laminates used on a number of very different boats, in the hope that these case histories will give the reader some idea of what might be appropriate on a particular boat, both as a basic laminate and as reinforcement for some weak area.

4/ Preparing the Hull

You can forget about trying to grind and wash away every trace of foreign material from the wood. We regularly lay up our coverings right over any paint that happens to be on the boat. We do no sanding, except to fair off any prominent ridges or bumps on the hull, unless we were unlucky enough to run into something that reacted chemically in some strange way with the resin. It happened once, when building a fiberglass mold on an epoxy-painted hull. It didn't disturb the laminate; it simply turned to a gooey mess beneath it that we knew would wreck the surface of our mold and possibly stick it to the plug. So we had to strip off everything down to bare wood and start over.

This "wooding" is not only a waste of time, but in the case of antifouling bottom paint, it amounts to throwing away a good poison for rot bacteria that is already in place. So the preparation of the hull amounts to little more than knocking off any marine life, large paint blisters, rust flakes, or proud seam putty, and grinding down or planing off any unsightly angularity in the planking.

If there are gouges or depressions in the hull, it

would be good to fill them with resin and talc putty. However, if the gouges are extensive and you intend to fasten without pre-drilling, then don't use putty. In this case putty will turn the fastenings away, and you don't want large areas that are not closely fastened. You can fill large depressions with fastened-on patches of fiberglass, so that these areas are pre-fastened. Another solution is simply to cover the gouges with the regular covering, if they are shallow enough, and then putty the depressions left on the outside of the covering.

Small depressions and faint bumps are no big worry, since they tend to diminish as you add layers to the covering. This is the natural result of rolling out the material; the roller fails to squeeze hard in the depressions and compresses most on the bumps. That's the good news. The bad news is that wetting out and rolling fiberglass is a knack that takes some learning. All but the most expert operators tend to build their own bumps and hollows as they work the wet materials. Matt is the most difficult to lay up smoothly. Undoubtedly one of the reasons so many boats are covered with cloth is the ease of its relatively smoother job. But cloth does little of what a hull needs; and if this book does nothing more than to persuade you to forget about glass in the form of cloth, it will have been quite worthwhile for both of us.

There are other preparations you must make before you can begin the actual laminating. First, all through-hull fittings should be removed, to be reinstalled later over the fiberglass. This is the best way, because its flange will then clamp the edge of the covering to the hull. Nor does it present any problem on most boats, except that the added thickness of the hull with the covering in place may require a longer-necked through-hull. Sometimes there is a backing block on the inside of the planking that can be removed and either left off or replaced with a thinner block. Otherwise, a shallow depression in the planking, as deep as the thickness of

When possible, remove all metal fittings and replace them after the fiberglass covering has been put on. (Milton Silvia photo)

the covering, might keep the total thickness within reach of the fitting. (The fiberglass in the depression will be stronger than the missing wood.)

In addition to the through-hulls, all hardware items on the hull, from bowsprit shroud plates to zincs, should be removed and replaced over the covering (more about this later). Take off stem bands and other metal rubbing strips, boarding ladder brackets, exhaust flanges, rudder heel fittings, cutlass-type or flax-packed stern bearings, propeller shaft struts and intermediate bearings. The treatment of most of these should be fairly obvious, but it's necessary to discuss the details and variations in handling rudders and underwater propulsion gear.

When a rudder or propeller shaft projects from what is essentially a hole in the hull, open to the water, you have to decide whether that shaft alley or rudder port is sound and tight. If it is metal lined or of a wooden construction that you trust for the foreseeable future, all you need do is clamp the fiberglass terminating at the edge of the hole with a well-fastened metal ring or flange. However, if you have a potentially leaky alley or port, by far the best cure is to fabricate and install a fiberglass lining tube. Bore out the alley or port if necessary and hook on to the tube with the fiberglass on the exterior. On the interior, the tube can have a flange on which to bed a flanged stuffing box, or it can be laid up around or bored to fit around the horn of the box. A better procedure than the old-type flanged stuffing box is to clamp the hose of a flexible rubber-necked stuffing box right onto the fiberglass tube where it comes out of the wood on the interior.

Almost all boatbuilders lay up these fiberglass tubes by wrapping glass cloth around any sort of mandrel with the right diameter. But one word of caution. Watch out for metal or one-piece wood; you'll never get it out after the fiberglass shrinks tight to it. Instead use cardboard or polyvinyl chloride (PVC) tubing and wrap the cloth until you have built up the thickness wanted. This has always made a strong tube. We were very pleased with such tubes until one boat's shaft got so out of line that it rubbed against the side of the tube so hard it wore away the resin. The shaft got hold of the cloth and unraveled enough turns to jam itself tightly in the alley and bring the engine to a dead stop! (See what I mean about cloth? It *peels*!) Truthfully, we still use cloth when we need its great strength in a thin wall, but since that episode, we always wind on a few layers of matt first, so that the inside of the tube won't be caught up by the shaft, and you can lay to that.

When you remove a propeller shaft strut from a hull, you have to remember that it must be reset later on

Note that fiberglass is wrapped over the base and around the leg of the propeller strut (upper left-hand corner). The rudder port (the bronze tube just above the rudder) was similarly wrapped. (Milton Silvia photo)

the same shaft centerline, or it won't line up with the shaft log and engine. Unless there happens to be a shim under the strut pad that can be eliminated or thinned down, you will want to make a shallow depression in the hull where the pad sits to allow for the thickness of the covering laminate. It is wise to rout a little deeper than needed; building up extra glass is easier than grinding it away and makes a stronger job. The depression should also be generously larger than the pad, to allow for the thickness of the material turning in over the edges of the depression. After the strut has been reinstalled, any depression left around the pad's edges can be evened out with polyester putty.

It may not be necessary to make a depression for

29

the base of an intermediate bearing or strut, one used to steady a long shaft between the shaft log and the main strut. Provided that you can reinstall the strut with new bolt holes slightly aft of its former position, you can line it up with the shaft where it sits on top of the laminate. This is usually affected by where the new bolt holes would come out on the inside of the boat.

Unfortunately, it is not uncommon to find that a new set of fuel tanks, or something equally troublesome to remove, has been built in on the inside of the boat over the strut bolts and has made them quite inaccessible. You might even be faced with removing an engine or two, or part of the cockpit sole. If such is the case, or if you are reluctant to remove, reinstall, and realign a strut, it is usually possible to cover over the pad and wrap the laminate around the strut's leg for a couple of inches. When the resin cures, it will shrink tight around the leg, making a watertight seal. If at some time the strut does have to be removed, the fiberglass can be chopped off. Frankly, I don't like this approach as well as having the strut bolted over the fiberglass, because I fear that it could cause more damage to the hull if the strut was struck in just the wrong way in an accident. But covering the base of a strut certainly is quicker and cheaper in a tricky arrangement, and it should remain strong and tight in service if the leg is well wrapped.

On motorboats whose rudders have heel fittings, and sailboats that may have other bearings along the rudder post as well, all such fittings should be removed and their lodgings cut deeper to allow for the thickness of the laminate. When the rudder is close to or fits into a concave aft face of the rudder post, that surface must be cut back, not only the depth of the single laminate that will be on it, but twice that if the rudder is also to be covered.

Covering a wooden rudder is relatively easy, and very reassuring because of the strength it adds when the metal stock is bound tightly to the blade. The watertight seal of the covering will be vastly improved if the wood is notched back from the metal wherever the stock leaves the wood — at the top, bottom, or at an intermediate bearing if it is a full-length shaft — so that the fiberglass can be wrapped completely and solidly around the metal at these points.

All metal fittings that are reinstalled on the boat should be well bedded around *and into* the fastening holes. One serious disadvantage of fiberglass (as compared to wood) is that its hardness requires a clearance hole to get bolts, lags, and other smooth-shank fastenings through it, to say nothing of through-hulls, depth finder stems, and similar sizable fittings. Each of these holes, therefore, creates a potential leak without the all-forgiving "goo," such as 3M's #5200, Sikaflex 241, or other bedding compounds. Only stainless steel self-tapping screws can be driven into a tight hole in fiberglass, which makes them the first choice for refastening small items through a covering. Even these should have a dash of bedding of one kind or another.

Because the fastenings can eventually be knocked loose and create small leaks, we believe in minimizing applied hardware on the hull, especially below the waterline. The most common victim of this philosophy is the "stem iron" or band. This lovely, traditional bronze protector for the face of a wooden stem is superfluous when added to the doubly thick layers of fiberglass wrapped around the stem. It only complicates repairs after severe impact, so it's common sense to leave it off.

5/   Terminating the Covering

Second in importance to fastening fiberglass mechanically to a wooden boat is the treatment given to any edges of the material. It would be an ideal covering that had no edges, one that was an unbroken skin over every inch of the outside of the boat. But wooden boats are rarely shaped like footballs (at least much less often than fiberglass boats), and some of the areas into which their surfaces are naturally broken up — decks, tops, house sides, and cockpits — may have no need of covering.

When only the hull is to be covered, your first thought might be to bring the fiberglass to the deck edge and then cover the raw edge with a trim or rubbing strip. This is like taking a shower with your mouth open. No matter how well the strip is bedded and fastened, water is likely to trickle down behind it some day and either lodge on the edge of the fiberglass or sneak in behind it. If this were only salt water, it wouldn't matter. If the fiberglass were well fastened, little would come of a slight dousing of the area. But fresh water, good old gentle rainwater, or even dew, is something else. All it needs is an edge on which to rest or the slightest pocket in which to settle, or just two surfaces between which to cling as a film, and it may create damp spots that stay damp long enough for rot to take hold.

To eliminate the chance of dampness being trapped by the edge of the covering, don't cover the edge over — tuck it in. The safest place to tuck it in is under an overhanging rabbet in solid wood, so that water would run down over the turned-under edge and would have to run uphill to get behind it (which doesn't normally happen). When the laminate ends this way, it need only be well and closely fastened. Covering it with one kind of trim or another might be all right, but it's not necessary.

On a boat with an existing rubbing strake or guard rail, then, that part does not have to be removed and reinstalled over the laminate when only the hull is to be

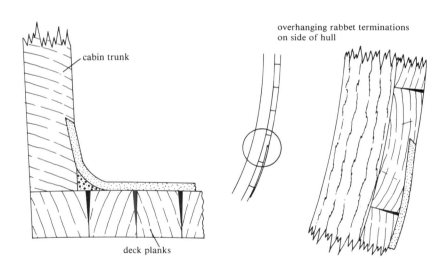

cabin trunk

deck planks

overhanging rabbet terminations on side of hull

Fresh water doesn't need much of a surface to cling to before it collects and gives birth to rot. To eliminate the chance of dampness being trapped by the edge of the covering, tuck the edge in under an overhanging rabbet (a beveled recess) in the solid wood. Water would have to run uphill to get behind the edge —an unlikely event.

covered. It is actually a better job if the covering ends in a rabbet, the undercut top edge of which is as close as possible to or right at the bottom edge of the strip.

It is another matter entirely if, in addition to the hull, the deck is going to be covered. Then the only sensible arrangement is to have the deck covering come down over the top of the hull covering for a perfect seal. When a deck covering joins a hull covering, the treatment of any toe rails or guard rails is a matter of preference. They can be removed and refitted on top of the fiberglass, or they can be left in place and covered over. In general, it is less expensive to cover large rails that have a lot of curve than to remove and reinstall them; it protects them, too.

It is not easy to retain the crisp look of a wood rail, however, since the fiberglass layers tend to soften both in-corners and out-corners and make fair lines wavy. Without diligent rolling and patient sanding and filling, the original nice shape can become a lumpy mess. Just one more reason why a layer or two of glass cloth (or worse, Dynel) is so attractive to the dilettante: it's so much easier to do a good-looking job with cloth or Dynel than to do it right with matt. Of course, we do not use roving where there are many tight corners, such as in covering a small rail, because it is so stiff it will try to bridge the corners. We do insist on at least two layers of matt on all covered surfaces. Use a couple of layers of lightweight matt if you want. But remember that cloth will not remain tight when abused, and that nothing is more subject to abuse than the rails of a boat.

On some boats with bulwarks that are topped by railcaps, you can have the best of both worlds. You can remove the railcaps, cover the bulwarks with fiberglass, and put the wooden caps back on over the covering. If the caps are so intertwined with chainplates and other hardware that they will be ruined and cost a fortune to replace, you may be able to cut a rabbet into their overhanging edges, or into the bulwark and up a little into the bottom of the cap. It is important that the laminate extend above the level of the bottom of the cap, so that you keep the water from running under the cap. The water might come to rest on bulwark wood that is enclosed by fiberglass on both sides, where the wood is much less able to dry out.

More often than you might think, we have an owner who wants only the bottom of his boat covered. This is the area that has usually deteriorated the most and is likely to cause grief by leaking. Also, as discussed in Chapter 2, a hull covering has the least effect on trim and performance. Further, it is often cheaper than other jobs, although the bottom is more difficult, so cost is not always proportionate to the areas of topsides and bottom. If you choose to cover only the hull, tuck the top edge of the covering under a rabbet that runs along a certain plank above the waterline, as described earlier in this chapter.

If you are, on the other hand, an owner who wants to cover only the topsides (probably for cosmetic reasons), then you should also end the laminate in a (plain) rabbet in a certain plank (properly called a strake, unless the boat is planked with full-length planks). The reason for not crossing seams, if you can help it, is that these can never be caulked past the edge of the covering, and you will have to stopwater each seam. The stopwater, if needed, should be a softwood dowel driven into a tight hole that is centered on the intersection of the seam and the edge of the covering. When the dowel swells, it will seal off the seam where it passes under the covering. You can then continue to caulk and putty the seams right up to the stopwater without the water making an end run around your work.

6/ Turning the Hull

A most important operation in covering a hull is turning it. Resin is a liquid — although a viscous, sticky one — and glass is heavy stuff. Laminating overhead, then, while not impossible, is extremely difficult. A surface that is vertical is not bad. One that leans out toward you, as on a flaring bow, or turns under, as at the bilge, gets more and more tricky to cover as it moves off the vertical.

The only sensible thing to do is to turn the boat as much as possible in order to save large amounts of time and difficulty in covering the areas that would otherwise be overhead. This is so important, and the difference in the time, effort, and quality of the work is so great, that the best thing to do when possible is to turn the boat upside down. Unfortunately, with most boats over 30 feet, this is highly impractical; high, fragile deck structures, engines to be removed, tanks to be emptied, and heavy ballast keels can make flipping your hull impossible.

But any boat that can't be turned over can be laid over on one side and then the other. It won't hurt most boats a bit as long as the low side is supported in several places, or over a large fore-and-aft area. Once in a while we do get a boat whose structure is so loosened up that there is a real danger of its shape being distorted just from having part of its weight resting on the turn of the bilge. If this is the case, we cover the topsides while the boat is still upright, carrying the fiberglass down around the turn of the bilge as far as possible below the area on which she will rest without getting into a paperhanger's nightmare. When enough layers are in place around the bilges, they will take the weight without damage. It might take a total of six or eight layers, or in a really devastated area, 10; but once the basic four are fastened on and have cured, it is surprising how much stiffer the structure becomes.

Sometimes a wobbly keel can make it ticklish to lay a boat down on one bilge. The plank-on-edge keels of stock motorboats are notoriously weak, but we have also seen old sailboats with startlingly limber keels of both the planked-down and the wooden fin or dead-wood types. A loose keel can be covered on both sides, carrying the laminate up into the deadrise before tipping the boat. Or, as the boat is tipped, we can shore her up along the garboard area with blocking or jacks, to keep her weight off the side of the keel until it has been locked in by the laminate.

A good hefty laminate with numerous sizable fastenings through most of its thickness will really freeze the keel in place. Therefore, it is very important that the keel be as straight as possible while being covered. Admittedly, this is hard to check by eye when the boat is lying on its side. If we use a large bevel square, or make a pattern of one side and try it on the other, the angle of keel to deadrise can be checked from side to side. Because a boat's bottom can sometimes be distorted, it is important to check again with a careful look at the boat from each end.

Travelifts and cranes can lower a boat on one side and raise it again very easily, no matter what its size or weight. We have done it the hard way many times with boats over 40 feet and 15 tons with an ordinary six-ton hydraulic jack and a few piles of blocking. The operators of lifts and cranes are in charge of what they do, so we'll only make some suggestions about the jacking and blocking. You might need this advice if the man in charge of the jacking is an amateur, or if he did *not* learn his trade in a rural boatyard before machinery was so common. (See Appendix for more details.)

When using only one jack to tip down any boat, it is important to estimate the location of the fore-and-aft center of her weight. Make sure that there is blocking on which the keel rests both as far forward and aft of the center of weight as possible. While we can easily do this on motorboats, we are limited on deep-keeled sailboats to the length of the bottom of the keel. Fortunately, most traditional sailboats have keels with a relatively straight bottom extending way aft of the center of weight, although often only a little forward of it. With extreme fin-keelers, such as are common in fiberglass today, it is not safe to jack them down with fewer than two jacks plus two blocking piles. It is fortunate for the business of tipping boats onto their bilges — and for the nervous systems of boat coverers — that the other extreme fin-keel craze, before fiberglass, was so long ago that the wooden boats that had them have all but disappeared. But while there is some worry about the bow or stern wanting to swivel with short traditional sailboat keels, there is comfort in the fact that from 30 to 50 percent of the entire weight of the boat is in the ballast keel itself, sitting right on the keel blocking. If you place your jack between the forward and aft keel blocks, and as nearly at the center of the weight of the hull as you can estimate, there should be little bow-heavy or stern-heavy tendency.

On a sailboat, the center of weight of the hull is almost always just about at the center of weight of the ballast keel — a close enough estimate for the purposes of jacking. With a motorboat, you have to think a little more carefully and figure where the engines and tanks are located. Find the probable location of the center of displacement, which *is* the center of the boat's weight; it varies considerably with the type of boat. To stay out of trouble, position a stout cribbing or blocking pile about one-fourth of the way in from either end of the boat. This structure can be torn down or built up in one- or two-inch increments as you jack her down or up. If anything goes wrong, the boat will almost immediately come to rest on these two piles, which are also used to support the boat while you readjust the jack for another bite. A couple of big, broad, low-angled wedges are handy to fine-tune the height of the blocking and to help you get every last fraction of an inch out of the jacking process.

When a boat is up straight, she is so perfectly balanced that you could hold her there with one hand. As she is lowered down on one side, the weight pressing on her ribs can increase to between one-third and one-half of the total displacement of most sailboats, and more than that on some motorboats. Of course, this depends on how far down the boat is tipped; but, again, the farther the better for efficiency in laying up the fiberglass. It is crucial on models with a flat bottom aft to put the turn of the bilge practically on the ground, as low or lower than the bottom of the keel.

Since an enormous number of pounds per square inch would come to bear on one tiny area of the planking, you should never use the jack directly against the hull. Instead, you should use a plank or timber set fore and aft along the hull, which has *at least* one inch of length for every foot of boat length, which is wide and thick enough not to bend much, and which is either sawn to a curve or built up with a wedge at each end to roughly fit the fore and aft curve of the hull. Not only such a timber but a metal plate between it and the jack may be needed on a heavy boat to keep the top of the jack from sinking into the wood. Likewise, a stout

In order to cover the underbody, it is necessary to tip the hull to one side. Here, Brownell stands support the hull during covering work.

block of generous area will be needed under the jack to keep it from sinking into the ground if the boat is not on a solid floor or pavement.

Brownell adjustable boat stands greatly facilitate lowering a boat from the upright position to within about two feet from the floor, which is the minimum height of the lowest of these boat stands. We always use several of them in lieu of the hydraulic jack in the upper sector when tipping a boat. We are lucky that we live and operate in the town where they are made, and we have stands of all the available heights at hand.

Anyway, if you go at it slowly and deliberately,

keeping a couple of good cribs of blocking built up to her at all times, you can tip a pretty big boat down or back up in a half-dozen man-hours. While she is heeled way over, be kind to her planking and ribs. Let her rest on as many support areas as possible, carried as far toward the ends as possible. Make a special effort to support the stern, which is the part most likely to twist out of shape.

Just one more thought on the subject of jacking. If your boat has acquired a hog — which means that her ends have sagged due to lack of adequate support over the years, both afloat and ashore — it may be possible to fix her. When she is dry and loosened up, jack up the ends, letting the middle hang from them until the sheer returns to its original, saucy curve. Then, by fiberglass covering as much as you can of the topsides and the turn of the bilge before tipping her, you can hold the restored shape. A word of caution: this procedure takes time. You should increase the upward pressure slowly at the ends, keeping it even athwartships so as not to twist either end. Be gentle and patient. You don't want to break her in half, and you can't expect to reverse the settling of many years in five minutes. However, unless a lot of new fastenings and wooden parts have been added since she hogged, she should show marked improvement in a few weeks. What goes down must come up, unless it has been locked in place with a lot of new construction.

7/ Laying Up the Hull Covering

Laying up fiberglass is one of those activities you won't really understand until you've gotten your fingers sticky doing it. But a few pointers from those who've been in it up to the elbows can certainly ease the learning process.

The necessary prelude to lamination is cutting the glass. Hand lay-up cannot be done efficiently without having the glass materials precut roughly to size and piled neatly in sequence of use. It is no great chore to measure for the pieces to be cut, because you are not trying to fit the pieces precisely to the boat or to each other. You're just cutting enough pieces to cover the area you're working on, plus a little extra.

Suppose your boat is 35 feet long, beamy, and high sided. You have decided, because the topsides would be difficult to reach when she is heeled way over, that you will put four layers on her *from the deck edge to the waterline area* while she is upright or nearly so. You then plan to cover from the waterline area down across the bottom of the keel after she is tipped all the way down. For the topsides in this case, cut a layer of matt that will reach about a foot below the waterline, a layer of roving that falls about six inches short of the first layer, then two more layers of matt that are both six inches shorter than the preceding layer. These layers will give you a topside laminate that steps back from one layer to the full thickness in a band about 18 inches wide along its bottom edge.

Unless you are experienced or have several helpers standing by, we strongly advise against trying to put up any of these layers in long fore-and-aft pieces. It is much easier on a steep surface to lay up glass in vertical strips, like hanging wallpaper. You might even be able to put it up alone if it is 38 inches wide, if the surface is not overhanging, and if you are a quick-learning, deft, unflappable type. Each of the four layers, then, will be made up of many vertical strips of the material — approximately 12 strips of 38-inch width if the hull is 35 feet on deck.

Measuring for these strips is simply a matter of marking off the hull's topsides lengthwise (vertically) at intervals as far apart as the width of the material and roughly measuring the long side of each space. This will give you the number of lengths to be cut from the roll. Ideally, glass cutting is done on a table, at one end of which the rolls of matt and roving are hung on pipes, from which the material can be pulled out to lie flat and be cut off with a sharp knife. But you can manage with a pipe rigged up on sawhorses and a sheet of Masonite or plywood on the floor to cut against.

After you have cut one course of matt and one of roving for one side of the boat, and piled them where you can quickly pick off each as needed, it's time to set up a resin station and go to work. The resin station starts with a generous-size piece of waste pasteboard, such as a flattened carton, on the floor or ground close by where you'll be working. On it place a five-gallon pail of resin, your catalyst bottle and measure, several 2½-quart containers (called "paper pots"), brushes, rollers, stirring sticks, another five-gallon covered bucket with a gallon of acetone in it (where brushes and

Working toward the port bow. Note the resin station in the foreground. The dark bucket contains uncatalyzed resin; in front of it is the gallon jug of catalyst with its measuring pump. The white bucket contains brushes and rollers immersed in acetone; the #10 tin can has clean acetone for washing hands. (Milton Silvia photo)

rollers will be washed and stored), and some clean cotton rags. The brushes should be cheap, 3½-inch, wood-handled versions. Rollers should be 7 inches, with nubbly textured sleeves for rolling the laminate and fluffy ones for applying resin; handles and spool ends should be wood or plastic so they won't dissolve in acetone or resin. (See Appendix for more details.) This is your on-the-job supply station. By the end of the day it will likely be one messy piece of pasteboard, no matter how neat you normally are. That's why it's there: to protect your materials and intercept gooey, glass-fuzzed hands and tools, and dripping pots contaminated with catalyst.

Man your station and pour resin from the five-gallon bucket into two or three of your 2½-quart pots until they are three-fourths full. Catalyze one of the pots with 12 cc or ½ ounce of catalyst and stir well. Don't splash! (If you should get a spatter in your eye, run for the hose or faucet and flood the eye copiously with cold water; if it doesn't wash out right away, get to a doctor as quickly as possible.) Take the pot of catalyzed resin and a brush or fluffy roller and paint the surface where you'll be hanging the first three or four pieces of the first (matt) layer. After you find out how long the resin takes to set up in the temperature, humidity, and light conditions (sunlight is crucial) for the time and place where you're working, and figure out how long it takes to put up the pieces, you may want to paint farther or not so far ahead of where you're working.

It is important to paint the surface with the catalyzed resin before putting up any piece of glass material, because the resin comes through from the back and speeds up the wetting out. It is also important to paint ahead when you're putting up vertical or

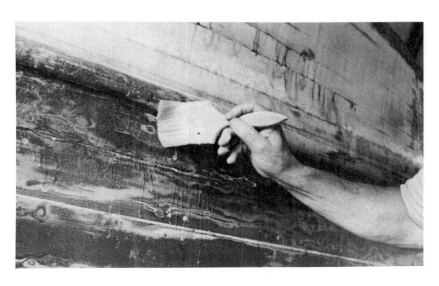

The surface to be covered must be wetted first with resin. (Milton Silvia photo)

overhanging glass, so that the resin will have started to gel and become sticky when you get there. It is much easier to lay up glass on resin that has reached the sticky stage. Once you have tried it both ways, you'll be inclined to go away until the surface gets sticky, rather than battle with glass that's falling off as fast as you can push it back up.

I wish I could tell you exactly how much catalyst to add or subtract for each variation in temperature or humidity and each brand of resin you might encounter. But my men and I worked for years under all kinds of conditions with many brands of resin, and all we know about cure time is that "you never know." You can ask your supplier for a bulletin that will tell you in what period of time a given percentage of catalyst will cause a given resin to "gel" and to "cure" (gel is like stiff jelly, cure is 95 percent hardened) at a certain temperature. But this is only a rough guide at best, because it assumes controlled conditions. On a damp, chilly morning, you lay up with that mix and it won't "go over" for half a day. By afternoon, with the sun streaming down on the job, if you use the same mix on top of an already gelled or mostly cured laminate, it will be sticking to your roller before you can finish rolling it out. Sure, after a while you can guess pretty well what to start out with, but you'll have to adjust to conditions almost every new day — and again as the day wears on and the weather changes, indoors or out (but especially out).

What this means is that you always should be checking on your mix. The ideal time in which to have the resin gel is from ½ hour to an hour after it is mixed. This gives you time to use up what you mix, which should never be more than one 2½-quart container per man applying it at one time. That way, you won't waste any if the job is slowed down for any reason. If the resin starts to gel in the pot, you'll have to throw it out. Dump it on a rock, or on plain dirt or gravel, out of doors: it may get burning hot, and it may give off a stringent, choking smoke until it cures and cools off.

DON'T leave half-full, catalyzed pots of resin lying around.

If resin shows no sign of gelling in an hour, you should double the "shot" of catalyst; if it still doesn't gel, give it three times as much catalyst. If it gels faster than you can use up a pot, cut the catalyst in half; if it is still too fast, use only one third as much.

You will find that you can't work under a burning hot sun, because the resin will gel faster than you can roll it out, and it will trap gases, which will form blisters under the partly cured surface. Nor should you work when fog or mist is wetting the working surface, because moisture will spoil the adhesion of new layers and inhibit the cure of the uppermost layer. Rainwater will also wash away uncured resin, so quit working far enough ahead so that the resin will cure before it rains. If caught by a shower, throw large sheets of polyethylene or Mylar over any uncured portions. These materials don't stick to resin.

You probably will start at the bow, although there's no special reason for that, aside from boatbuilders' habit. Place your pot and brush and a 7-inch roller within reach, and pick up the piece of matt you cut for your starting piece. If you have a helper, one of you can have the roller in one hand while you both put the piece up. Holding the material by its top edge, fit that edge up to the deck edge, or into the rabbet if you have cut one. Press it into place with the palms of your hands. When the edge is in position, spank, rub, and roll it into the resin with one hand, pressing the weight of the rest of the piece against the hull with the other hand just below. As soon as the top seems to be sticking, bring the hard roller into action, holding the glass up and against the hull with one hand as you roll downward with long, fast strokes of the roller. The idea is to get as much material as possible stuck to the surface, before the weight of what is hanging causes the whole thing to peel away.

This moment of putting up the glass is the critical

Left: *Putting up the matt.* **Below:** *The matt sticks well in tacky resin. (Milton Silvia photos)*

and frustrating one if you are alone. It's only half as bad if you have a helper and perhaps a third as bad if you have two. But don't be discouraged: I have seen two or three very accomplished old-timers lose a piece now and then when the surface has quite an overhang. If all else fails, you may have to use smaller pieces. After all, if it's small enough, you can just smother it until it stays there. But, usually, if the glass you have rolled into place will stay long enough to allow you to pick up your pot and brush and wet it out, the wetting can only improve the sticking.

When wetting matt, don't drag the brush or fluffy roller on it, or you will soon be dragging the matt along, too. You should ladle the resin on by dipping the brush and putting as much as you can on the glass with one short, flooding, forward-and-back swipe; then dip again. Hold the pot close under the brush at all times to catch drips. Always wet out from the top down, working with gravity, not against it. We might mention here that if this first piece is at the bow or stern, you can leave it hanging out past the face of the stem or transom several inches and trim it roughly parallel to that face. Then, when it is wet and limp enough, this overlap can be wrapped right around. A different approach, probably easier for a novice, is to end the topside layers short of the stem or transom face, each staggered back a little farther, and then cap the stem or corner of the transom with separate pieces later.

After a while, you will get a feel for how much wetting you need to do. When you think there is enough resin on the glass, put down your brush and roll back and forth and up and down with your hard roller, starting at the top and working down. The purposes of rolling are to press out any air that is trapped under the glass, to spread the resin evenly through the glass, and to squeeze out excess resin wherever the glass is floating in a too-thick coating of it. The rolling must be accomplished before the resin begins to gel, and with a

Above: *It is usual to roll out from the top down. (This is the second layer of matt over the fastened-on layers. This layer is staggered about 6 inches to the right of the edge of the first layer.)* **Below:** *If you don't want the resin dripping on you from your brush, wet out from the bottom up. (Milton Silvia photos)*

roller that has no gelled resin on it. Otherwise, the roller will pick up the glass and leave a hairy surface behind. Some workers like grooved aluminum rollers; we like the disposable sleeves on a wire frame with a texture like a hard, nubbly rug. Roll from the center of the piece toward the edges, to push the air out. If wrinkles in the matt seem stubborn at first, they will usually disappear when the piece becomes thoroughly saturated and the strands slide together. If a wrinkle persists, cut along its ridge with scissors to allow it to flatten as its sides overlap and blend.

If you get into trouble, it will most likely be due to tackling a piece that is too large, to overcatalyzing the resin so that it "kicks over" (cures) too soon, or to taking too long to wet out and roll down a piece. If the gelling time runs out before you're through working the glass, you are in a bit of trouble. To avoid problems, don't tackle a large area, catalyze the resin for a short gel time, or catalyze extra resin until you have the experience to hustle the work along accordingly. Little if

*It's getting smoother.
(Milton Silvia photo)*

anything is lost by putting on two pieces with a 10- or 12-square-foot area rather than one piece twice as large.

You can go on to the adjacent piece when you have wet out and rolled the first one. Depending on how long it took, and the condition of your tools and hands, you might want time out to wash tools and hands in acetone, and perhaps to catalyze a fresh pot of resin. (If you want a cigarette, go away from the resin and even farther away from the acetone, which is extremely flammable.)

All of the tools that you get smeared with resin must be washed with acetone from time to time while in use to keep them from getting gooked up with resin that will eventually turn solid and make them useless. When not in use, the brushes and rollers are stored right in the covered five-gallon pail with a gallon or two of acetone in it at all times. But brushes and rollers should be washed out before they are put in. The proper way to do this is to dip them in the acetone in the storage bucket, then hold them off to one side of it, perhaps over a waste can, and work the resin out of the brushes with your hands, or off a roller or scissors with a brush. Dip again, and repeat until clean.

You must get the resin out, because it will harden and ruin the tool, even under acetone. You should not wash off the resin into the bucket, because it will settle to the bottom and harden in a cake — in which all of the stored tools are "frozen" and ruined. The acetone in this storage bucket should be added to as it gets low, changed after every few days of constant use, and replaced completely before the tools are left in it for a weekend or longer.

After you have washed all of the tools, then you can re-wash your hands in the nice, clean acetone in your three-pound coffee can. Here again, dip out some acetone with cupped hands, and wash where resin and glass fibers won't drip back in and contaminate the supply. Otherwise, your hands will always be slightly sticky. Have a clean rag handy and wipe your hands while they are still damp with acetone. But you'll have to be quick about it, because the stuff evaporates like crazy! (See Appendix for alternatives, safety tips.)

When you put up the second piece, you should butt it against the first piece to make it easier later to get a good finish on the hull. The compound curves of the surface might cause a small gap between adjacent edges, but a gap, which will eventually show up as a faint depression in the surface of the laminate, is easy to fill with resin-based putty, which is watertight. An overlap, on the other hand, will show up as a ridge that will have to be ground off to achieve a perfectly smooth surface. If you have a workboat and you want the most strength for the least cost of materials and don't mind the ridges, go ahead and overlap the adjacent pieces. But don't overlap, make ridges, and then grind them down. This only takes you back to the same amount of protection and strength provided by staggered butts in all layers. In fact, if you grind big ridges too vigorously, you might go right through both of the last two sealing layers of matt.

In the end, butting all of the pieces in the laminate makes a great difference in the fairness of the laminate, and therefore in the amount of work required to achieve a yacht finish. Since there is three to four times as much labor as material in a covering job, costwise, it is cheaper, if you are worried about the strength and watertightness of a given number of butted layers, to add an extra layer or two to the laminate than to try to fair its surface after overlapping all of the pieces in it.

After you have put on two or three pieces of matt, go back and bring the roving layer along. Of course, you can continue all the way to the other end of the boat and then go back and put on the roving, but practical considerations usually favor working the two layers together on any but the smallest boats. First, it saves the time of moving the materials, tools, and any staging

53

back and forth. Second, it is easier and more economical on resin to put up the roving while the matt is still wet, or at least sticky. But, most important on larger boats, the roving and matt will cure more or less together, reaching the right degree of hardness and surface dryness to be fastened at the same time. The first piece of roving should be narrower and shorter than the first piece of matt. For reasons of strength and watertight integrity, the seams in one layer of the laminate should be at least six inches away from the seams in other layers.

Roving is hung, wet, and rolled in much the same way that matt is done, except that roving wets out more slowly and can be pulled around to remove wrinkles without a tendency to tear. In fact, you couldn't break its strands if you tried. The strands of roving are stiff and springy; they resist being bent into or around sharp corners, and you can waste a lot of time trying to force them into a place they're trying to bridge. If you need to run roving around a corner for its strength, you should soften the corner: round outside corners and fill inside corners with a triangular piece of wood or a radius of putty. If the corner is a stem face or a transom edge that needs to be strengthened yet should also be crisp, you can build it back to sharpness with matt at the end. But if the corner is not structural, such as a guard or toe rail, cut the roving short of it and do the sharp parts with an all-matt laminate.

As soon as any parts of these first two layers of matt and roving are dry to the touch and have a firmness similar to pasteboard or leather, you can begin fastening the layers to the hull. This may happen as soon as an hour or two in hot, dry conditions. On the other hand, in chilly weather you can do a whole side in one day and staple it the next morning before you put on the next two layers. I can't tell you how it will be — just that the surface must be dry enough not to gum up the stapler too much (which you must then rinse with

Above: *Putting up the bow piece.* **Below:** *Tearing down — parallel to the stem. (Milton Silvia photos)*

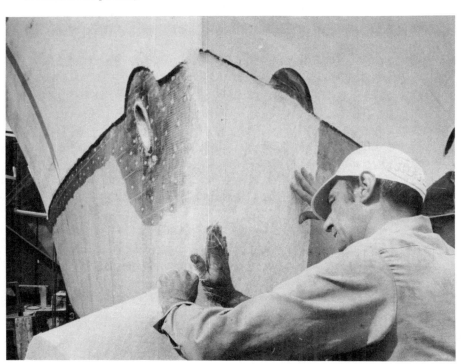

Wetting out the bow piece. The container of resin is held close under the brush in order to catch the drips. Note the tapered depression around the starboard hawsepipe that will allow extra covering thickness. (Milton Silvia photo)

acetone and re-oil, not forgetting to remove any staples first, for acetone dissolves the glue that forms them into a "stick"). Yet the fiberglass must not be too hard to penetrate, or the staples will do a split and stick their toes back out of the surface. Trying the stapler only on the surface will tell you whether it's ready or whether you've waited too long.

As I already have indicated, the ideal tool for this job is a power stapler, air-driven or electric (if powerful enough), that drives a heavy wire staple. You might be able to rent one of these tools from a tool rental shop, wooden box factory, packager, pallet builder, building contractor, or even a wooden-lobster-pot builder, since power staplers have been used widely to build pots lately. At the same time, there is nothing wrong, as mentioned in Chapter 3, with galvanized asphalt shingle nails or bronze ring nails (like Anchorfast). In fact, you can use any fastening with a wide head and stout shank, including flathead screws. Common sense tells us, however, that thin coverings on light, wooden hulls can get along with relatively lightweight fastenings, but that thicker, stiffer coverings on massive constructions should have fastenings of heavier wire.

Unless the planking is very soft wood (and even when it is), nails and screws hold much better when driven into a drilled hole that is between one-third and two-thirds of the shank diameter. The harder the wood, the larger the hole should be. To find out what holds best in your boat, you can drive in several sample fastenings until their heads are no more than one-eighth inch from the surface, then test the holding power of each with a claw hammer or wrecking bar. It is not likely that you will get most fastenings so well planted that they will snap off before you can pull them out, although it certainly is possible with some fastenings in planks that are hard enough and thick enough to have allowed you to bury a good length of shank. What you need is stiff resistance to a good hard pull, so that you

The young man at left uses an air-driven stapler to fasten the layers on the starboard side. In the foreground is a portable compressor. (Milton Silvia photo)

58

are assured, in your best judgment, that the glass and wood will not separate when well sprinkled with fastenings every few inches.

When staples or nails are used without drilling, it becomes important to drive the fastenings before the fiberglass gets hard enough to turn them away. Once you've had them bounce back, you won't forget to fasten at the right time. If you do have to drill, use either a tapered drill or a stepped hole made by a big drill with a stop on it and a smaller drill for the rest of the hole. Any sort of nail or screw can be made to penetrate and hold well through the hardest glass; it's just an awful lot more work.

Whatever fastenings are used should be almost as long as the thickness of the planking, but not long enough to come through on the inside of the boat. The spacing of the fastenings has more to do with the thickness of the laminate than anything else. For the "basic four" layers of laminate, ⅛ inch thick, the fastenings should be about 2½ to 3½ inches apart in all directions. As the laminate gets thicker, the fastening pattern can be spaced more widely, but they should be no farther apart than 4 to 5 inches at ¼-inch thickness, 6 to 8 inches at ⅜ inch, or 12 inches at ½ inch.

When fastening, space staples close together in all directions. (Milton Silvia photo)

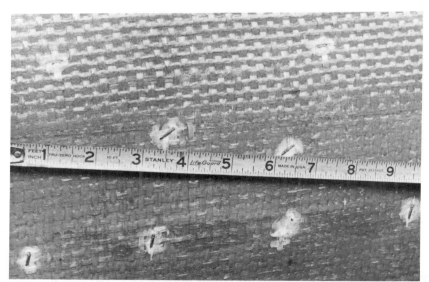

The previous remarks about fastenings are not more specific because each job needs its own study of what ought to be used. To make a judgment you need to bear in mind the purpose of the fastenings: to hold the covering and the boat together — *forevermore.* This they can do better than any glue. But to realize the full potential of mechanical fastenings, you have to use fastenings with good holding power and keep them close together. Don't think ''good enough for now''; think ''forevermore.'' On a planked boat, you naturally will want to keep fastenings out of the seams — other than that, what you will need is a random pattern that leaves no large areas unfastened and an extra-close row along the edge of a termination or parallel to a corner.

As soon as the fastenings are in place, you can go on with the laminate. This is the time to add any patches of extra layers that you might have planned to put on over a seam along which there are cracked ribs, over some loose planks or butts, or over a stove-in area that has been filled in with short pieces of planking before covering. These patches of extra laminate (which would be alternate matt and roving unless the area had corners too sharp to accept roving) also could have been applied to weak areas *before* the first two fastened-on layers were started. If you are worried about these weak spots being distorted, or even broken, when the boat is tipped out of plumb (and we have covered boats whose condition was that delicate), you may have to get these areas built up and well fastened before starting the general covering. However, if the patch is but a few layers on a generally sound hull, you are ahead of the game if you can apply the patch after the first two fastened-on layers are in place. This way you will not waste time on a special fastening session for them, as you would if they were put on first. Even a very heavy laminate that needs some extra-heavy fastenings is better applied on top of the fastened-on layers when possible. This is because of the fastenings under the tapered edges of the extra buildup that was done before drilling became necessary. This way you will need to drill holes only for the heavy fastenings that you want in the thick part of the reinforcement.

After any extra local layers come the two final sealing layers of matt. Before you put them on, it is a good idea to look over the hull and grind off any bumps or ragged edges that might otherwise telegraph their presence through the final layers to the surface. You might also find some disturbing depressions that weren't noticed on the hull's surface or that have developed in the laminate. These can be built up with small pieces of matt made to fit by tearing their edges to the profile of the depression, which causes the edges to blend into the surrounding surface. But sharp, relatively deep holes might be leveled off more easily with a dash of body putty.

We usually add pigment to the resin used in the last two layers — we use the color that will be used to paint or gelcoat the boat. Most workboats that we cover, and a few pleasure boats, too, go out with a glaze coat of the same pigmented resin or of gelcoat over these pigmented layers. Done for economic reasons, this is a rather rustic finish, to put it mildly, but it will last for several years without care. When the owner does do some refinishing, it will get smoother with each painting if some sanding and surfacing precedes each coat.

It is not necessary to use pigment in the resin of the last two layers when you intend to smooth extensively with putty and then use a paint or gelcoat finish. If you are not experienced in fiberglass work, it would be just as well if you didn't use the pigment, since pigment in the resin masks air bubbles under the matt, and it takes an experienced eye to detect and roll these out when only their faint shape, not their color, indicates their presence. On the other hand, pigment in the resin and the putty is a nice touch, because it backs up the finish color and takes the glaring contrast out of scratches and gouges. Whether or not you pigment the resin or putty, and whichever system of finishing you have in mind, you should continue to use the same low- or no-wax resin in these sealing layers. You should use it because any last-minute patches, a glaze coat, and possibly even the bottom paint can go right on without sanding.

A good technique in fitting the final two layers, one that assures a smoother surface, is to tear or comb the edges of the pieces where they butt. Tear a narrow strip off the straight-cut edge of the matt as you would tear a piece of paper; or comb the last inch of the edge outward with a comb or brush of sharp steel pins not more than ¼ inch apart. You can make this device with finish nails set in wood if you can't buy one. Either way, you leave a fuzzy edge that, when meshed with a similar edge on the adjacent piece, can hardly be detected after rolling.

Getting back to your hypothetical boat, you have now laid up the basic four-layer laminate, with perhaps some patches of reinforcing layers somewhere within it, on the topsides. If this had been a six- or eight-layer laminate, the only difference would have been more alternate layers of matt and roving between the fastened-on two layers and the final sealing layers. Your job now is to tip the boat down on one side and do the bottom in the same manner that the topsides were done, butting each layer to its topside counterpart in that stepped-back area along the waterline.

Of course, you might have decided to use more than the basic four on the bottom, or to increase the number of layers by steps as you approach the keel. You might want to tear the top edge of each layer so that it won't leave a ridge, since nothing will be butted to it. However, where a laminate exceeds 10 layers, a covering approaching ½ inch in thickness, you should be thinking about some stronger, drilled-for fastenings to complement its greater strength and rigidity. Believe me, if you are putting that much fiberglass on a 35-foot hull, anywhere but on and under the keel, you're going to have a very strong boat!

In the past few years we have patched a number of fiberglass production sailboats longer than 35 feet that had less than ½-inch thickness in the sides of their keels or deadwood. Not only were these keels hollow, but there were hefty lead ballast castings inside of some and bolted to the outside of others. One of these backed out of a slip — that's all — and holed the keel on a rock. Another bounced once on a ledge. But with all that wood in your boat, even wood that is a little brittle with old age, she might not have holed ½ inch of glass, and she certainly wouldn't have flooded fit to sink like those fiberglass boats did.

No matter what weight of glass is used on the keel, we always carry its full thickness across the bottom from each side, effectively doubling its thickness there. Our reasoning is simply that that's where she sits when ashore or aground, and also where she is most likely to strike bottom. This doubling is also a simple way to terminate the laminate in a place where it is not so awkward to work or difficult to keep track of the more sophisticated methods of blending the layers of the two sides. However, when the keel is very narrow, rounded, or even pointed along the centerline, we cannot effectively use such an overlap. Such cases call for a number of U-shaped layers around the bottom of the keel, stepped back into the hull layers on the sides of the keel. There is good reason to use some of these U-shaped layers on any keel, just to guard against water penetration where the layers of one side overlap the other. But, again, it is most important on narrow keels — ones whose bottoms are not wide enough to give at least 3 to 4 inches of overlap.

Another thing about keels is that they're almost always sitting on some number of blocks. Obviously, you will have to step your laminate back where it is too close to the blocking or actually pressing into it; then, after you have straightened up the boat for the last time, you can jack up the keel, shift the blocking, and fill in any uncovered places.

Rather than interrupt the running account of how to apply the covering, I left the ways to handle through-hull fittings and hardware bolt holes until now. Obviously, if a through-hull is not going to be used again (and you do find a surprising number of abandoned through-hulls on older boats), you should remove it, plug the hole with wood or fiberglass putty and run the covering over it. It is also likely that you will find that new construction has buried an old through-hull, so that getting at it on the interior requires dismantling too much joinery. You can drive a wooden plug into it and cover it over; or, if that would leave an objectionable bump in the covering, you can hacksaw the flange off flush with the hull first.

But the question was what to do about the holes for those fittings that were removed and will be replaced over the covering. Provided that the hole can be reached from the interior with a hole saw or an electric drill, the easiest method is to cover over the hole with the covering, then drill it out afterward, using the hole on the interior of the wood as a guide. If that is impractical, there are a couple of other ways to work from the outside. One way is to trim off the fiberglass flush with the inside of the hole with a narrow-bladed, sharp knife just when each layer or pair of layers reaches the pasteboard or leather stage in hardening. If you miss that stage, you may find yourself using a drill and a round or half-round file instead of the knife — annoying, but no big problem. When you do such trimming, you should cut on the push stroke of the knife only, since dragging it back may lift the green fiberglass from the surface, and such delamination will not heal itself after the resin has reached this stage.

Another solution is to plug each hole with a waxed wooden plug, which is left projecting from the hull at

Trimming the matt around the keel blocking. (Milton Silvia photos)

Above: *Patching an area left uncovered at a keel block. The jacks in the background support the keel where it has already been covered. Steel plates spread the jacks' pressure (approximately 15 tons on the two jacks).* **Below:** *To ensure good wet-out under the keel, it is necessary to turn the matt up and saturate its back side before turning it under. (Milton Silvia photos)*

least the thickness of the total laminate. Each time you go by with a layer, you snip the layer with a scissors and lay it up against the plug. When finished, you grind the whole business flush with the surrounding surface (it almost always builds up higher), then drive out the plug. This last method is more trouble than the others, but it is often the best way to handle bolts whose holes cannot be re-drilled from the inside. It is about the only way to handle blind holes like those for lags and hanger bolts such as are used on stern bearings. Bolts also can be left in place, waxed up, and any exposed threads wrapped with masking tape to keep them clean.

Speaking of stern bearings: if this is the stuffing box type, or if no work is required on the shaft alley, it will not be necessary to remove the propeller shaft. You have only to slide the stuffing box back on the propeller shaft, cover it and the shaft well with masking tape and paper, and lay up your covering on the surface of the stern post. Trim it at the edge of the alley, slide the stern bearing back in place on top of a gasket or bedding of wet matt, and apply gentle pressure with the strut bolts until the fiberglass hardens. This makes a firm base for the bearing that aligns it accurately with the shaft. It is

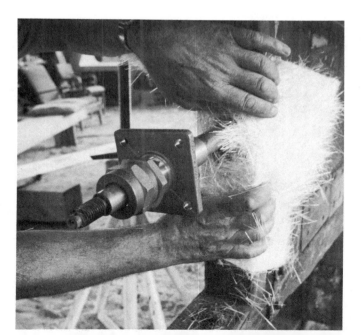

The fiberglass covering goes right under the stuffing box. (Milton Silvia photo)

The stern post being covered. The stern bearing will be slid back in place over the covering in two or three layers of wet matt cut and fitted like a gasket. (Milton Silvia photo)

by far the best way to reinstall such bearings and stuffing boxes, as long as the alignment was all right when they came out. You can always tell whether a stuffing box or a rubber shaft bearing is aligned with the shaft by looking at the ends of the latter to see that the shaft is not squeezing against one side. Rotate the shaft by hand in either case, after making sure the engine is out of gear and lubricating the bearings with water, with perhaps a bit of soap in it. If the shaft rotates easily by hand, there can't be drastic misalignment. (If the shaft rattles in the bearing or stuffing box, it needs repacking or a new rubber insert, as the case may be.)

Although my men and I have never found it necessary to use masks or gloves when working with fiberglass and resin, a few builders have an allergic reaction to the materials. If you are not certain whether you may react adversely, spend some time in a fiberglass boat shop and find out for sure. (See Appendix for safety tips.)

8/ Covering Decks and Tops

WHAT TO USE

Since fresh water is what ruins a deck, the exclusion of water should be uppermost in your mind at all times when planning the covering. If your deck is sound and strong, you will not need as much glass on it as on your hull, but a really watertight, durable job may require more glass than you might think. The absolute minimum deck covering that can be expected to remain intact and watertight is two layers of matt, the first layer well fastened. Two layers of lightweight matt can be used on a small, lightly constructed deck. Use at least two layers, and use matt, not cloth. (After you have done that much, you can put on all the cloth you want. It won't do any harm, except add a little weight.)

I stress the minimum limit of two matt layers because, while decks in general can survive with lighter laminates than hulls, this is usually carried so far that most covered decks are inadequately protected. There are several reasons for using deck coverings that are lighter than hull coverings. First, the deck is not usually subject to as many deteriorating forces as the hull, so unless the weather and subsequent rot have been allowed to get into it, a deck often will be in better structural condition than the hull it's on. Second, the deck is not normally subject to the same potential pressures, strains, and impacts as the hull. For example, it almost never will undergo the shrinking and swelling of a dry-to-saturated cycle, once made watertight, and neither does it, one certainly hopes, ever sit on the ground. Third, it is important to the performance of almost all boats to keep the deck as light as possible. Fourth, it is much easier and less costly to beef up a deck that needs strengthening with wood than it is to do wooden repairs on a hull. On some decks, nothing more than an overlay of well-fastened plywood can restore ample rigidity before the covering goes on.

Not that we haven't at times put ¼ inch or more of laminate on a deck where we thought that this was the most effective covering, with regard to strength, durability, cost, and performance. Sizable cruising boats and workboats, particularly fishing boats, are certainly better off with a thick laminate on their main decks. When such a laminate is well fastened, it adds tremendous strength to any type of deck structure. However, the decks of most boats in the size range where you would use the basic four layers on the hull will be adequately covered with three or four layers of matt, which will weigh from .6 to .8 pound per square foot.

If your deck shows no sign of "working," if it is a plywood deck with well-strapped butts, or made of tight, stoutly fastened strips of natural wood decking, then you can leave woven roving out of the laminate. For a sound deck, all you need to do is to increase impenetrability to water and wear resistance, to the greatest depth that weight and cost considerations will allow.

If, however, the decking has been "coming and going," if it consists of relatively wide pieces, if its seams will no longer stay tight or its fastenings are suspect, then you should put woven roving back into the laminate, at least in the fastened-on portion. Remember, roving is best for tying things together. Its great tensile strength will keep a deck from twisting. At the same time, roving will build up the stiffness of the laminate and will decrease trampolining in a springy deck.

PREPARING THE DECK

Much of what has been said about preparing the hull for covering also applies to decks. It is not necessary to remove paint, for the covering is to be fastened on. You shouldn't necessarily bother to rip off an existing covering that is in decent condition. You certainly should, however, grind off an old covering where it is lumpy, and punky spots ought to be dug out and filled with wood or body putty, and saturated with preservative before covering. An existing covering will often be fiberglass cloth, which your fastenings will penetrate

"If it moves, remove it; if it doesn't move, cover it." This view shows the cockpit sole, the coamings, the engine hatch coaming, and the house all covered. (Milton Silvia photo)

easily. With some sanding to bare its surface, the old cloth should hook right onto the added layers. As we say around the shop, "If it moves, remove it; if it doesn't move, cover it."

TREATING HARDWARE AND TERMINATIONS

If at all possible, hardware should be removed and replaced with ample bedding over the laminate; if not, its base should be wrapped tightly or a metal binding plate should be well bedded and screwed down over the edge of the fiberglass. I prefer metal because of its low profile, because it can be removed and rebedded many times without destroying it, and because it will not shrink, swell, or deteriorate.

Where the covering of the main deck can turn down onto the side of the hull, or where the covering of a trunk or top ends by turning down onto the sides of the structure, you won't have a potential water trap. If the covering overlaps other fiberglass, all the better. But where the laminate ends coming down over wood, any trim pieces used to cover the edge of the laminate must be wholly on the fiberglass (not half on the wood) and well bedded to prevent rot.

However, where you are bringing the deck covering up against the side of the cabin trunk or a hatch coaming, the worst thing you can do is to cover its edge with a trim piece. Whether the covering ends at the corner or turns up onto the vertical surface an inch or more, edging it with anything like the ubiquitous quarter-round molding is creating a natural water trap. There is nothing quite as secure as taking the deck laminate up into an overhanging rabbet in the vertical surface. If you cut a clean rabbet a little deeper than the thickness of the covering, put a narrow extra strip or two of glass in it to beef up the edge of the covering, and use closely spaced fastenings, you'll have a termination that sheds water like a duck's back. It will also look so neat that there will be no reason to cover it up. If I possibly can, I use the overhanging rabbet everywhere a covering terminates looking upward. (See page 33.)

When you come to a deck hatch coaming, you can be sure it will never leak if you go right up the sides, over the top, and down the inside. Of course, you may have to cut back the ledge or rabbet around the top edge where the hatch fits, or rout the inside edges of the hatch itself, to allow for the thickness of the added fiberglass. Otherwise, the hatch may jam. If the coaming is varnished and you want to leave it bright, then your choice is either to cut an overhanging rabbet low on the sides or to remove the coaming and replace it, well bedded, on top of the deck covering.

As for the hatch itself, if you cover it, you can just cover its top and sides and trim the glass flush with the bottom edge. Fiberglass shrinks as it hardens, so it should pull very tight around the hatch. Even if you wanted to, you probably couldn't get the hatch out of a two- or three-layer laminate without damaging it. But if you want to make sure of that, just cut a shallow rabbet ¾ inch to 1 inch wide along the bottom outside edge,

Fastened-on first layers on a hatch. Roving was not used on this stout construction. (Milton Silvia photo)

73

build this back with a strip or two of matt until it is flush with the surface again, and then bring your covering down over it.

Cockpit coamings are a problem if they are too thin for a rabbet. The choices in that event are either to go up and over, trimming the laminate flush with the bottom edge on the inside, or to remove the coaming and replace it over the fiberglass covering. Some coamings do not sit on top of the deck but are fastened against the side of the opening to a carlin that supports the deck edge. Over an open cockpit, canvas was often turned down between the deck edge and the coaming. You can do the same with your fiberglass covering, bedding the coaming well when you replace it.

SOME DIFFICULT AREAS

There is nothing better from the point of view of protection than to cover all of the surfaces on and above the deck; but many deck structures, especially motor yacht deck houses, flying bridges, and cockpits, are so complex that they try the abilities of the most expert carpenter-and-glassman team. It is up to you to decide whether you should attempt to cover some of these very busy areas. Fortunately, the trunk or house sides, windshields, and coamings of older boats and of high-grade younger boats are built of solid, natural wood, which lends itself to ongoing repair with fitted pieces of the same and to rabbeting for main deck coverings turned up into it. Such solid wood in a vertical surface can often be left uncovered safely. It is usually only the more recent, cheaper, production craft, whose plywood sides and tops are blended with laminated softwood styling curves, that get to be such a mess that covering is the only hope of saving them. Interestingly, the reason most of these structures are such a mess is that they were originally covered with glass cloth, or with vinyl, which is worse.

*Yes, even the quarter
bitts are covered.
(Milton Silvia photo)*

If there are bronze opening ports that open inward, there may be a bronze finishing ring on the outside that fits around the horn of the casting, the tubular projection that extends through the hole in the wood. You can remove the finishing ring, run the covering up against the horn, and reinstall the ring, well bedded. If you want to eliminate the ring, you can do so by beveling the wood inward around the horn of the window with a chisel to make a V-shaped rabbet against it. Resin-saturated strand roving wrapped around the horn in this rabbet will shrink tight to it, making both a seal and an anchor for the edge of the covering. Some boatbuilders fit the horn of the portlight neatly through the wood and don't use the finishing ring. In that case, you will have to use the rabbet and strand roving, unless you want to buy or make finishing rings.

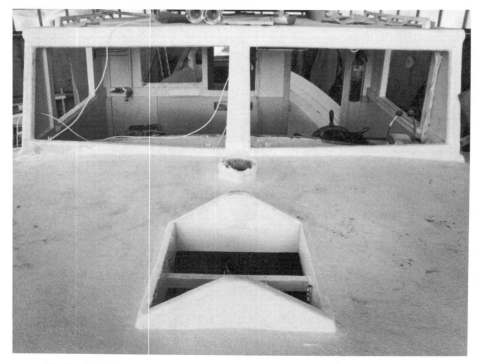

Deck, skylight, and windshield are covered. The mast collar is built into place. (Milton Silvia photo)

Some opening portlights, most deadlights, and many aluminum-frame fixed windows do not have a horn. These are listed by suppliers for outside installation, and when so installed they can be removed and replaced over the covering. But some plain, flanged lights or windows may be installed on the inside, leaving the edges of the opening in the wood exposed. In this case, your best move is to turn the covering into the opening and trim the edge of the fiberglass flush with the inside surface of the wood, so that it meets the metal flange of the reinstalled window. To do this without making the opening too small, you often have to enlarge the opening all around by the thickness of the laminate.

Many older motorboats have windows that drop or

crank down into a recess in the house sides. Since the recess is usually metal lined and provided with a scupper to drain outboard, it is enough to turn the covering inward around the edge of the window opening and let the water run into the drip pan as it always did. If the pan has deteriorated, well, there's a chance for you to practice your newly acquired skill with fiberglass. A glass pan will never corrode.

Those windows that slide in metal channels lined with fuzz and nylon are often a mess because of the dirt that has collected in the trough or pocket in the house side that contains the track. The dirt not only tends to plug the drain holes through the sides of the house but also holds moisture against the wood for long periods. Two options for treating this problem are: (1) You can turn the covering in around the edges of the opening and trim it off flush with the inside face of the wood and leave things as they were, except for any cleaning out or repair of the trough and track. Or (2) You can take apart the entire arrangement and line the trough completely with fiberglass. This is really biting the bullet, since it calls for patient, fussy work to build a completely watertight liner in place in the trough and then either up the sides of the window recess to the top or into an overhanging rabbet a little way up each side. It is also probable that if you cover the interior of the trough, you will have to enlarge it, making it deeper and wider to allow for the thickness of the laminate. You should not proceed to build up a laminate in the trough until you have made sure that there will be enough clearance for the window and its track when you reinstall them.

If you have to cover the wooden parts of pilothouse forward windows or windshields, you will need considerable patience and ingenuity. Even if they are sound and don't need covering, you will want to turn the trunk top covering into an overhanging rabbet well up on the vertical surface, perhaps just under the windows, to prevent deterioration of the always susceptible house-to-trunk joint. If you want to cover the window rails and other joinery, you should remove any fixed windows and carry the covering into the rabbet so that it will end behind the glass. You will no doubt have to cut back the sides of the rabbet to keep the opening big enough to receive the glass again. You probably will not have to increase the depth of the rabbet, because you will be building up the surface that is rabbeted just as much as you are building up the bottom of the rabbet. Opening pilothouse windows that are set flush, hinged at the top, and bound with flat metal that covers the seam can usually be removed and reinstalled over the fiberglass.

FLYING BRIDGES

If you want to cover a house top that has a flying bridge on it and you are not going to cover the bridge, you should first check whether the bridge can be removed or lifted up readily. The covering will be easier to do and to get watertight in way of the bridge if it can pass under the bridge uninterrupted. If the bridge was definitely not built with removal in mind, you will have to see that the covering of the house top is properly terminated against its inside as well as its outside surfaces. This requires an overhanging rabbet in the sill of the bridge around the outside. Around the sheltered interior where rain won't be falling on it, you can safely turn the fiberglass up off the deck a little and cover it with a bedded molding.

Should you intend to cover the bridge as well, then the bridge laminate can overlap the turned-up house top covering. The problem of how to terminate the fiberglass then moves up to the top of the bridge. Probably there will be a molding or railcap around the top that can be removed and reinstalled over the fiberglass or rabbeted for it.

The inboard or console surfaces of some flying

bridges are quite complex, what with steering columns, instrument panels, compartments, seats, and lockers. To make matters worse, many are constructed with plywood on the outside of a light frame, with wings that usually have plywood on both sides of the framing. It is difficult to cut clean rabbets into plywood, and it is dangerous to its strength when the plywood is so thin that there are only one or two plies whose grain spans the cut. Further, you will have to use short fastenings in thin plywood wherever it is not trimmed or backed up with thicker wood.

To do a good job of covering a flying bridge, then, you will have to tailor the laminate, its fastenings, and its terminations to the configuration and construction details of your particular bridge. Fortunately, on these surfaces, which suffer little physical abuse or stress, you can safely use three layers of thin matt as a basic covering. You will need additional reinforcing layers only on those joints or corners that might, or already do, "work." But flying bridges are more exposed to the destructive effects of sun and rain, and less often favored with a dose of mildly antiseptic salt water, than any other part of a boat. No wonder they are almost the first place we see rot breaking out on boats that have been let go. Therefore, it is very important that you concentrate on watertight integrity, good scuppering to drain away potential pools of standing rainwater or dew, and good ventilation of any closed-off parts of the structure.

COCKPITS

In studying decks from rails to flying bridges, we bypassed one most important area, the cockpit. Whether your boat is a sailboat with a small footwell or a powerboat with more cockpit than any other kind of space, that area is a catch basin for rain and spray and is much abused by foot traffic. If she should happen to be a workboat or fishing boat, her cockpit should also be able to withstand enormous loads and stiff blows by hard and heavy objects. Obviously, a workboat cockpit should be extra thick. It will also need to be very well fastened because of the jars and bumps and the flexing when loaded that will tend to shatter any resin bond it has established with the wood.

When my men and I repaired two of a well-known builder's fiberglass fishing boats, a 35-footer and a 55-footer, we were shocked to find their plywood decks covered with fiberglass not fastened down in any way. It was incredible, but this builder had built hundreds of decks with several layers of plywood *power stapled* together — and not a single staple in the fiberglass. (Equally incredible was the lack of glue between the stapled layers of plywood.) Yet these were fiberglass hulls built with barrels of resin, which is an excellent wood glue in the absence of resorcinol or other marine glue. It should be obvious that these stapled decks with their unfastened covering would be several hundred percent stronger and more durable with glued-and-stapled plywood and a stapled fiberglass covering.

A further problem with these decks' construction was that all of the several two- to three-foot deck plates were installed flush with the deck in a raw, rabbeted hole through the covering and plywood. The covering was not extended into the rabbet so that the deck plate ring could be bolted down on top of it. Naturally, the covering had already loosened and lifted, and the plywood was water-saturated in a wide area around each ring. A workboat deserves a better job on her cockpit.

Even if your cockpit is not a work area, its covering should be substantial enough to be scuffed, jumped on, and clouted without damage to its watertight integrity. The cockpit sole of a yacht should be covered with no less fiberglass than the main deck. If the construction is sound, you can use matt, but if the cockpit is coming apart at the joints or getting dozy, there should be some roving in the laminate. Should the weak areas be few and scattered, the roving can be applied in patches that span them with the fastenings of the covering set to include the roving in their grasp.

A wooden boat's gutters under seat and floor hatches are often pitifully inadequate. The shallow grooves and tiny scuppers have usually been long clogged with dirt that dams up rainwater and causes more damage than if there were no gutters. You can make bigger, deeper gutters of fiberglass, which, because of the thinner walls possible with this material, will take up no more space than the wooden gutters did. When these are in place, you can bring some layers of

A seat hatch gutter has been built in place with four U-shaped pieces, two of which slope deeply toward the inboard face, where they spill out onto the cockpit sole. (Their openings are out of sight in the foreground.) (Milton Silvia photo)

the deck covering right down into them and keep the runoff from ever wetting the wood.

If your wooden gutters have had it, you can make up fiberglass replacements on the outside of a waxed stick of wood with one edge well rounded, to form the bottom inside of the gutter. Such fiberglass gutters can be cut from a single long piece into four separate pieces mitered at the corners. When these have been fitted in place around the hatch, you can patch the joints together with matt. If you want to make the four sides in one piece, measure the hatch opening carefully, lay out and fasten four sticks as a rectangular mold on a sheet of plywood or Masonite, and lay up what will be similar in appearance to a hollow picture frame. Be sure to allow for the thickness of the outside laminate on all four sides, or the gutter won't fit into the opening without "cuttin' an' cursin'."

Of course, if the old wooden gutters are of ample size and still reasonably sound, you only need to cover them with a couple of layers of matt. These layers can be carried from on deck, into the gutter, and out again on the inboard side. Such layers can be carried right down into a good big scupper. Smaller through-hull drains should be removed, their recesses chopped lower to allow for the thickness of the covering and then reinstalled on top of it.

In some cases you might consider making up your own fiberglass tube with which to replace an old drain fitting. Such tubes are best made up over a mandrel of cardboard or PVC tubing, either of which is fairly easy to remove after the fiberglass has shrunk. (See the discussion of propeller shafts and rudder ports in Chapter 4.) A tube laid up around metal or wood will be just about impossible to get off unless such rigid cores are split lengthwise into two wedges that can be knocked free of each other, or unless they are otherwise arranged to collapse away from the fiberglass. Another way to make a tube on a hard mandrel is to lay up a couple of layers, slit them lengthwise while they are still green, knock off this split tube when it is hard, and finish the laminate without a mandrel.

You can build an integral flange on one end of a drain tube and hook the covering right onto it. On the other end you can clamp a drain hose leading to the through-hull. Alternatively, you can make a recess in the wood around the end of a tube and build up a flange around it on which to connect the covering. Of course, through-hulls as well as drain tubes or scuppers can be fabricated the same way. However, a through-hull and a drain should not be all one straight piece between cockpit and hull if there is the probability of movement of the structures that could lead to eventual rupture. Better to have a hose connection between them for flexibility.

On decks that have scuppers cut out through bulwarks or through the stern, it is usually a simple matter to carry the covering from inside through to the outside, and then turn it onto the hull covering. If the thickness of the laminate tends to restrict a small opening, the opening should be enlarged before it is fiberglassed.

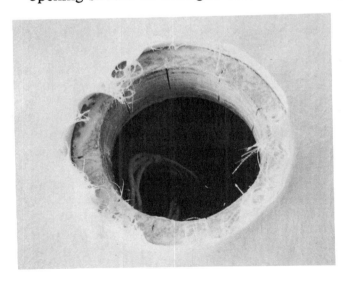

A wooden mold fitted over the mast hole forms a collar integral with the deck. The saw cuts in the mold allow it to be knocked apart easily to remove it when the fiberglass is hard. (Milton Silvia photo)

Planked-up bulwarks that have numerous stanchions and are not sheathed over them on the inside can be an awful chore to cover. It takes time and skill to do a good job of working the fiberglass into the corners and around all of the stanchions. If it is at all practical, sheathing over the stanchions will make a much easier and neater job. If the bulwarks are suitably constructed, you might be able to stuff the bays between stanchions with PVC foam brought flush with the stanchions' inboard faces. PVC foam is light in weight, tough, and easily cut with knife or saw — and fiberglass bonds unshakably to it. You can use short fastenings in the stanchions and long ones through the glass and foam; or you can put fastened-on patches of glass in the back of the bays and stick the foam to these by pressing it against them with a layer of wet matt between. Don't forget that you will want the bulwark covering rabbeted up into the railcap just as much as you would the hull covering, unless the cap is to be removed and the top glassed across to join the two coverings. Even then, a railcap that is rabbeted is stronger and less likely to develop rot from dampness lodged beneath it.

The nicest thing about covering decks is that all of the walking surfaces can be pigmented, rolled-matt surfaces. Wet out the final two layers of matt with resin pigmented to the color you want, and roll them out with a nubbly roller. Like canvas of the past, this is a natural-looking, textured, nonskid surface that will need nothing but scrubbing for some years. It not only wears well, but you can adjust its nonskid property toward smoothness in waterways and dirt-catching corners by taping off those areas and filling the surface with a glaze coat of the same resin. Of course, you can also add more nonskid texture in the form of fine sand in the resin on a work area, at the anchor-handling station, or around the foot of the mast. But for walking on yacht decks, in general, a rolled-matt texture is just about right.

UNDERLAYING AND SANDWICHING

I should mention the common practice of putting down a layer of plywood on an old wooden deck before covering it, which you may have seen done or been advised to do by one of the "expert" repair advisers every do-it-yourselfer seems to collect. The plywood underlayment is used for four reasons by those who want to cover their decks with thin layers of fiberglass cloth, vinyl, or canvas: (1) The plywood is dimensionally stable. It is much less likely to shrug off, bunch up, or split a thin fiberglass covering by its shrinking and swelling than natural wood. (2) The plywood is clean, bare wood, so the thin, unfastened covering will bond better to it than to an old deck. (3) The plywood covers the seams, holes, and bumps in old decks, making the covered surface come out relatively smooth and fair. (4) The plywood is expected to add some stiffness and strength to an old deck that is "working" due to wasted fastenings, over-caulked seams, or incipient rot.

Now, unless you started reading this book in the middle, you know that for the purposes of a substantial, fastened-on covering, only the third and fourth reasons for using a layer of plywood under it could apply. You do not need to worry that the deck planking will disturb an appropriate laminate (this eliminates Reason 1). Nor do you need to worry about the bond of the fiberglass to the deck, since you will be fastening it on (that eliminates Reason 2).

But a deck with a very uneven surface might be most quickly made fair with an underlayment of plywood prior to covering. Likewise, if your deck is very weak, you might want to add strength to it with a thoroughly fastened-down layer of plywood. Plywood is lighter in weight and lower in cost than the extra-heavy fiberglass laminate that would be needed to restore physical strength and stiffness to an alarmingly tired deck. Further, two or more thin layers of it glued together will have enough stiffness and shape memory to restore missing strengths in beams, too. If the beams are weak, don't use one thick sheet. Laminate at least two thin layers to form an on-deck beam.

Should minimizing weight be more important than cost, or should you want to retain high performance in a lightly built boat, you'll find that PVC foam makes a much lighter fairing or stiffening material to underlay than plywood. To get equivalent results, the PVC foam should be about 50 percent thicker than plywood for the same job. Even then, the foam will yield a sandwich that is roughly one-half to one-third the weight of one with a plywood core. Moreover, PVC has a low R factor, or high insulation value, which is most welcome on a deck in any climate. Two PVC foam boards currently available are trade-named Airex and Klegecell. PVC is much more expensive than plywood, but it makes an extremely impact-resistant, tough sandwich when fiberglassed on both sides.

To sandwich the PVC in glass, fasten or weight down the foam in wet matt on top of one fastened-on layer or more of matt. Then cover the foam with at least two layers of 1½-ounce matt, the number depending on the size of the boat. It's only the roughest gauge, subject to many modifying factors, but starting with two layers on decks up to 20 feet, you might add another layer for every five feet of greater length. One thing you have to do, if you use PVC on a deck, is to cut out a small area wherever deck hardware will be bolted through it and substitute a piece of wood, plywood, or even solid fiberglass. Otherwise, the foam would be crushed, the deck dented, and the bolts loosened by strains that tilt the hardware.

If you use plywood as an underlay on your deck, sprinkle it liberally with fastenings to the old wooden deck. I'd like the plywood bedded in glue, a polysulfide adhesive such as Thiokol, thick paint with preservative mixed in, or wet matt. That's my instinct, but I suppose that with enough fastenings, those who use nothing but a primer or preservative between deck and plywood will probably suffer only somewhat less strength and a deck that might be squeaky underfoot.

Only a small percentage of wooden boats have decks in such bad shape as to need underlaying or a sandwich construction. Usually the underwater part of the boat has fallen apart before her deck is in such dire straits, and a large majority of wooden decks that I have seen could be brought to excellent condition with a single-skin laminate of modest thickness.

There are other existing (and no doubt yet-to-be-invented) underlaying and sandwich materials. Masonite is used for underlaying and is relatively cheap, dense, hard, and durable. I have seen it survive for years laid wrong side up on the wooden decks of 30- to 40-foot yachts when bedded and well fastened. It was usually merely painted on top, and looked like a poor man's facsimile of canvas. When used under fiberglass, the fastenings of the covering should extend well through it, due to its layered, easily delaminated nature.

Balsa core is still the most widely used deck sandwich core. It is somewhere between plywood and PVC foam both in its cost and in the weight of the completed sandwich. Its position between two extremes and the rigidity that balsa core adds to a structure have much to do with its popularity. Because this material consists of many little blocks on a scrim, you should weight it down evenly all over in wet matt to get a good bond to the fastened-on glass. Although I have never tried it, you could instead weight down the balsa in wet matt on the deck. Cover it with at least one layer of glass, nail down the whole business, and then put on the final layers. Because the blocks are end-grain pieces, with respectable compression strength, there is usually no need to fit blocks of something else under bolted-on hardware.

BOLT HOLES

No matter how you cover your deck, an important factor in the success of the job will be the way you reinstall its hardware. Fiberglass is much more likely to leak than wood, for the simple reason that it doesn't swell tight around a bolt like wood does. Further, most bedding materials don't get a good grip on the slick and impervious surface of fiberglass, so that they are more easily separated from or washed out of the interface between deck and fitting. There are several things you can do to ensure tightness:

1. You can take the trouble to switch drills. Drill through the covering with a clearance hole for the bolt, then switch to a slightly smaller drill bit for the hole in the wood — one that requires driving the bolt with modest hammer blows, or spinning it in so that it threads the hole. This in itself makes for a fairly watertight fastening.

2. Roughen the surface of the glass under the fitting so that the bedding compound can get a grip.

3. Use a tough, sticky compound that stays flexible. There are too many excellent compounds for me to list every one. They start with good old white lead and run through oil-base products to the latest silicones, polysulfide adhesive sealants, and polyurethane adhesives.

My favorite compound in the latter group is 3M's #5200. This stuff not only dries to a tough elastic state, but it has such good adhesion that you will often need to cut through the seal to separate the part from the deck. We once jacked the forward end of a 10,000-pound boat off the ground trying to remove one of the Ideal Windlass Company's aluminum anchor-handling bowsprits from a fiberglass deck. Only patient sawing with hand-held hack-saw blades won the battle.

Another time, after removing about 50 seven-inch #20 bronze screws from a massive wooden toe rail that was bedded in 3M's #5200 on a 45-foot boat, we were forced to cut up the rail in little pieces and carefully chisel the last traces of it (and the #5200) off the fiberglass-covered wooden deck. That's why I trust the adhesion of #5200!

4. No matter what kind of goo you use, there's no security like a ring of caulking cotton around a bolt under the head before you drive it, and maybe another under the washer before you take up the nut.

There's nothing worse than a wet bunk. Most boatmen would rather live with a leaky bottom than a leaky deck. So watch those holes in the overhead.

9/ Finishing Techniques

FAIRNESS

Chopped-strand matt is of a fairly constant thickness, and roving is quite uniform. There is no way to lay up a fiberglass laminate by hand, however, without getting some variations in its thickness. During application, the glass will be floated more by the resin in some spots than others, and the matt will be thinned out in one place or bunched up in another by brushes and rollers. Experienced workers will do an infinitely smoother job than novices, but some undulations are inevitable. Therefore, no hull with glass laid up on it will be anywhere near as fair as a hull taken from a mold that was itself taken from a meticulously hand-faired hull, or "plug."

By "fairness" I mean the absence of hollows, swellings, ridges, or grooves, or any other discontinuities in the surface of the finished job. I am not referring to textural smoothness (the absence of roughness), which is a matter to be dealt with below.

Luckily, there is much you can do to make a covering job fair. First, you can see that the surface is as fair as possible before covering it. Grind off any putty that is protruding from the seams, grind down any plank edges that are raised or meeting angularly, and fill any large hollows or depressions as discussed in Chapters 4 and 8. Then, as you lay up the fiberglass, you can butt the edges of the material and/or tear the edges of overlapping matt to avoid creating ridges. Further, you can learn to wet out and roll down the matt carefully so as not to move it around too much. With the woven roving, you should stretch it out, smooth out any wrinkles, cut off any stray strands (or find a "home" for them), and roll the surface in all directions, like rolling out a pie crust, to level it as much as possible.

SMOOTHNESS

The surface texture of rolled matt is pretty rough — rough enough, as I said in Chapter 8, to make a nonskid deck. As resin hardens it shrinks, and the strands at the surface are left protruding somewhat as the level of the resin sinks below them. The resulting texture can be filled by application of various materials, including more resin, to be mentioned later.

At this point, someone is sure to suggest, "Why not use glass cloth, with its relatively fine weave, as a final layer? Cloth can be easily filled with a coat or two of resin, gelcoat, or paint."

That person is right. Cloth will make an easily filled final layer. There's just one problem: cloth will have little or no effect on fairness. If you are satisfied with the fairness of the covering as laminated, it is true that the quickest way to get through the finishing stage is to top it off with a layer of cloth. However, it is practically certain that in any laminate there will be undulations many times higher or lower than the thickness of cloth. If you intend to fair the surface, what is the worth of cloth that must be ground away or covered over? You might as well end the covering with your two layers of matt, grind off any previous bumps, and then fair the surface while you fill it. You'll save yourself the cost of the cloth, and your putty will adhere much better to the matt surface.

THE ART OF FAIRING

The most important asset you can have for fairing a surface is a good eye. If you can't see the humps and hollows, you'll never fair them out.

Somehow, it is extremely hard to teach most people that fairing is not plastering (and vice versa) and that they should not cover the whole boat with a thick coat of putty. To fair a boat, you need only fill the depressions. You are not fairing if you put the same amount of putty over the whole surface. A sure way to prevent overfilling is to try to keep the high spots bare of putty as you wipe down over the boat with your fairing tools.

I have made the mistake of assigning men to work on a boat after brief instructions in mixing and spreading putty, and not checking back soon enough to make sure they actually were fairing the surface. I learned the hard way that men can put on gallon after gallon of putty without improving fairness one bit! That goes for grinding, too. Grinding the covering all over for hours will make a lot of dust, and the operator certainly will feel that he has done a mean day's work — but he is likely to have removed unnecessarily a lot of good fiberglass and left in the unfairness. You should not grind a fiberglass-covered boat any more than you would grind a steel or aluminum boat to fair its rumpled plates.

You should go about fairing your covering job with a minimum of lost motion and wasted material. First, you will have to grind some — just enough to knock off any bold ridges, tufts, or lumps that are protruding above the general level of the surface. Further, the entire surface should get a light sanding if it has wax in it.

One good point about no-wax resin is that its tacky surface bonds very well to many types of paint and putty, and you can take advantage of that fact if you are satisfied to paint or fill the surface as laid up. Quite often we have painted a no-wax laminate directly with bottom paint. At other times we have applied putty directly to it. This means that you only have to sand the tacky surface enough to remove bad bumps. Even this much sanding will gum up discs, but if you use the cloth-backed type, you can wash them out with acetone. You wouldn't want to do this on a lot of surfaces, but it's a good shortcut to have in mind. It will work, for instance, on thin coverings over smooth surfaces where the laminate rolls out smooth enough to need only glazing with pigmented resin, gelcoat, paint, or some combination of these.

To get back to your fairing job, after you have ground down the bumps and sanded off the wax, you will want to do the actual fairing with putty. Putty for fairing, as opposed to putty for the final finishing, can be any good polyester-base putty. Auto-parts supply shops call it auto-body putty, and fiberglass supply houses call it hull putty or fairing putty. You can buy it in one-gallon or 10-pound cans, or five-gallon or 50-pound buckets. (See Appendix for more details.)

You can also make your own fairing putty by mixing talc with resin to a consistency that spreads easily but doesn't sag. Other fillers can be used: microballoons, Cab-O-Sil, ground glass, and glass spheres are a few of them. I don't suppose it matters, as long as it's an inert, durable substance that is not attacked by resin or degradable by the marine environment. It also needs to be fine enough to smooth out without a grainy surface, and one that won't crack from shrinkage.

Having tried many fillers, we have found that talc, which is cheap and readily available from paint manufacturers or their supply houses, makes a sturdy, fine-grain putty. It is actually finely ground soft stone, and it has no bad habits that I know of. It's not easy to sand, but neither are most of the other fillers. The addition of Cab-O-Sil makes putty hard and strong, but it is the meanest stuff to sand I have ever seen. The use of microballoons (actually tiny Bakelite spheres) is popular among those who wish to alter a boat's shape with thick putty without adding significant weight. This material is very light and quite tough.

Whatever you use for fairing putty, you should apply it in such a way that it will require an absolute minimum of sanding when it dries. You can spread it with the very wide, flexible putty knives that are sold by hardware and paint stores for finishing dry-wall joints. There are also some wider, flexible, metal straightedges and rubber-edged tools available. You will find these useful when you acquire the knack of wiping down over a wide area, holding them slightly bent with both hands to fit the fore-and-aft curvature of the hull. We have also used a ¼-inch- to ⅜-inch-thick board, 4 inches to 6 inches wide and 3 feet to 5 feet long, as such a flexible straightedge. A wide, rubber window squeegee held by its metal pole socket is another good fairing tool.

There is not much more I can tell you about fairing. It is, admittedly, a knack some people just don't seem able to acquire. At the same time, absolutely everyone has a good-enough eye to tell you when a surface is unfair. One suspects that the knack of fairing has less to do with the eye than with a willingness to do something about what the eye sees. But if you are one of the willing ones, perhaps a few rules will help you:

1. The putty knife and fairing tools are faster than the sander.

2. Better three rounds of putty than one of sanding.

3. Fair neatly: leave no excess that will have to be ground off.

The first application of putty should look like this — it should only fill in the depressions. (Milton Silvia photo)

4. The longer the tool brought down over the boat, flexing it to fit the fore-and-aft curve, the fairer the boat will be.

5. Because resin shrinks, you can hardly expect perfect fairing with the first round of puttying. It may take several applications to bring deep depressions up to fairness.

6. You can check fairness by bending a batten against the surface.

95

After several passes with the putty, the hull is all white and smooth. (Milton Silvia photo)

SMOOTHING THE SURFACE

Smoothing, as opposed to fairing, is a matter of getting the surface texture to a slick, paintable condition. Again, the hard way to achieve this is to just sand. This is not to say that it won't take a lot of sanding to arrive at a paintable surface. You should not try to smooth the hard surface of resin-based fairing putties, except for a relatively coarse sanding of obvious protrusions.

What you need for smoothing and finishing is a high-build, soft-sanding coating or primer. This will be a viscous, quick-drying liquid with which you can readily build up a thick coat. If you are planning to use paint for the finish on your boat, you can use a high-build primer that is compatible with the paint. If you are going to use gelcoat, or if you can't get a high-build primer for a given paint, then you should use a high-build, soft-sanding, resin-based product such as Mor-Bond.

Some of these finishing materials are for spraying, some for brushing. If you have no experience with a spray gun, I would advise you to use materials made for brushing. As for sanding the High-Build after it has dried, anybody can do an excellent job by hand with a sanding block. Most people do all right with a vibrator, and I know a few men who can do nice work, up to a point, with a belt sander. *Nobody,* however, should use a disc sander in this smoothing phase. The hard truth is that the most beautiful finishes on fiberglass boats are the product of hand sanding with the paper wrapped on a resilient or shaped block. That is why it is so important that at some point in the smoothing you switch over to a primer that is easily sanded.

THE FINISH

Just because your boat is covered with fiberglass, you don't *have* to finish the covering with gelcoat. Neither are you bound to use pigmented resin, which is a basic gelcoat without a filler to thicken it. Gelcoats do give excellent, long-lasting protection, but they are much more difficult to apply than paints on the outside of a boat. In this use they often need a lot of sanding and polishing, because they are not formulated to level themselves as well as paints. (After all, this is not an important requirement of their normal use in a mold.) Gelcoats can be doctored up to brush or spray on better than they will as formulated for use in molds, but you might be well advised to hire a professional boat refinisher if you want your covering job yacht-finished with gelcoat.

However, don't be astonished if a professional advises you to use a good boat paint instead of gelcoat. There are many excellent paints for use on fiberglass. I can't say that I know of any that weathered quite as well as gelcoat; but no finish on any boat that is used often and kept outdoors year round is likely to look spotless for more than a few years anyway. Therefore, there is a lot to be said for a paint finish, which is much more easily applied, touched up, and repainted than gelcoat. (See Appendix for more details.)

Brownell stands support the hull, which has been covered and is being painted.

If you find this hard to accept, it may be because you associate paint with wood and gelcoat with fiberglass. It is constant work to keep up any finish on wood, which is always breathing (changing its moisture content) and physically moving around. The opposite is true of fiberglass, which is relatively inert and not likely to shuck off any finish that is well stuck to it.

Of course, "well stuck" is a matter of degree. Gelcoat is basically the same material as the fiberglass body, so it becomes, ideally, an extension of the glass, which is as stuck as anything can be. Paint, on the other hand, may or may not become all that well stuck to the fiberglass, and that is why you should be sure to use a product that has been proven to do so.

What you have to decide, then, is whether to take on the much more exacting task of putting on and polishing gelcoat, which is more difficult to repair but should continue to protect the fiberglass for a long time, even after it looks terrible. The other option is to use paint, which will give you the best-looking job with the least work, is easy to repair, but will need repainting in a lesser number of years.

If you go the paint route, there is little more to be said here about finishing. This book is hardly the place to attempt to do justice to the vast store of painting know-how generally available. Besides, if you have long been the owner of your wooden boat, what I would say might be old hat to you or your boatyard.

Should you use gelcoat, you will have to learn to handle it. You have to sand, wet-sand, and polish it — or hire a professional to put it on — if you go for the ultimate finish that is possible with it.

Often a workboat owner has neither the time nor the money for a yacht finish, his only interest being a sound boat with which to get back to work. We have sent many boats back to hard service with nothing more than pigmented resin used in the final two layers of matt, glazed with another coat of the same pigmented resin. This is a rough-looking finish that hasn't improved our image with prospective yachtsman customers, but it is hard and tough in use. It stands up for some years, after which the boat can be covered with more of the same or with paint.

Dispersion pigments for use in polyester resin are sold in all colors by resin suppliers. Their cost differs with the color. It takes a rather small quantity of the pigment, less than a quart, to do a big boat. These colors can be mixed to obtain any other color or shade.

You can also use a small quantity of gelcoat mixed into the resin to pigment it in the final layers, or when glazing with it. A word of warning, however. You can mix dispersion colors together and different-colored gelcoats together, but if you try to mix a dispersion color into a ready-mixed gelcoat, it will probably separate either before or after application. Your finish will end up a mottled mess. So don't.

Unfortunately, the reasonable cost of achieving the physical benefits of fiberglass covering makes a really good finish on the job seem expensive by comparison. It would be nice to have a finishing technique that does as much for the boat for as little money as the covering itself does. We have been working slowly on this. However, you should bear in mind that while dings and scratches will happen, and colors will fade, the fairness and general smoothness of fiberglass will not change, once established. Further, the gelcoat or paint system on a fiberglass covering will last for a number of years, unlike a finish on wood (especially on an old boat), which can be virtually ruined in a season. The finishing of a covering, then, is actually worth its higher cost. As the years go by, you will save many times that cost, due to less frequent and less extensive refinishing.

10/ Waterlines, Centerboards, and Lapstrake Construction

Before you obliterate the painted waterline by one step or another of the covering process, record its location. I usually make a sketch of the boat and mark on it the distances from deck edge to waterline at several points along the hull. These heights can be taken a certain number of feet apart or their locations can be identified as directly below a certain chainplate, portlight, or other feature. If you are only covering the bottom to some point above the waterline, you can make a series of marks on the topsides above where the covering will end, but to simplify the task, use the same measurement up from the waterline for all of the marks.

If the boat has a boot top or stripe, you can either take a second set of measurements or, when the waterline has been restruck, mark off the boot top with a level and a block of wood. While a boot top may be the same vertical height above the waterline, its width has to change as the angle of the sides changes in order to keep its height constant. If you note the extreme width of a boot under a flat stern, you'll see what I mean.

When the hull is covered, and you have marked these waterline points on it, connect them with a wide, thin batten held in a vertical plane with only its top edge against the hull and on the marks. Held this way, the batten is a straightedge wrapped around the boat in the water plane that will help to straighten out the waterline. You will need more hands than your own two to hold the batten up, unless you're so independent that you'd rather drill holes in the fiberglass and nail it up.

If your boat's old waterline was good, the above instructions should help you keep it that way. As mentioned in Chapter 2, you won't need to raise it to allow for the added weight of the covering unless you have put on a tremendous amount of fiberglass, or unless the water level was already uncomfortably close to the painted line before covering. Bear in mind that the best-looking painted waterline is one that is well clear of the water and a bit higher at the bow than at the stern. If I had to make a rule about it, I would say that on a cruising yacht there should be a minimum of $\frac{1}{8}$ inch of bottom paint showing at the bow and $\frac{1}{10}$ inch at the stern for every foot of the boat's overall length. But the rule does not take into account the type of hull, the height of the topsides, the existence of a boot top, or any difference between the light and fully loaded waterlines. Take a careful look at your boat before you cover it and think about what, if anything, would improve the looks and practicality of its painted waterline. This would be the time to adjust it, if need be.

CENTERBOARDS AND THEIR TRUNKS

If the boat you cover has a centerboard, you have two additional decisions to make: what, if anything, to do about the board, and what to do about its trunk. Naturally, if either of these is built of nonferrous metal, you can forget about covering it with fiberglass. Should either be of steel, you might or might not want to cover it, depending on its condition. Even if both are of wood, you could not be blamed for putting off covering them, as long as there are no problems. However, it's not as difficult as it might seem to include the trunk in your covering, and it's downright easy to cover a wood or steel board.

On a wooden boat, if you decide not to cover either trunk or board, you can end the covering just outboard of the edge of the slot in the keel. You should not bring the glass quite to the edge, because you do not want the centerboard plucking at the covering as it travels up and down. If you want to go to the trouble, you can cut a rabbet around the edge of the slot and turn the covering up into it. But you should be putting a massive laminate on the bottom of a sizable keel anyway, and in one of these layers, you should be able to bury a close-spaced ring of flathead screws that will fasten it solidly to the keel.

A method that is good for a thinner covering on a smaller boat is to clamp the edge of the fiberglass around the slot to the keel with strips of metal — some screw-fastened bronze or stainless steel half-round or flat stock. The metal will provide wear protection.

You would certainly want to cover an iron keel, for cosmetic reasons as well as because the great tensile strength of the covering will supplement its keelbolts. If you don't want to continue the covering into a center-board trunk through an iron keel, then you will have to fasten the termination as described above for wood, using machine screws in bored and tapped holes. Use these fastenings over the entire iron keel if you cover it with fiberglass. When the covering is stoutly fastened to the wood immediately above the iron, there is hardly a way for it to get loose.

A lead keel does not need covering for its own sake. Unless you intend to fiberglass-line a wooden center-board trunk that exits through the lead, you might con-sider ending the covering near the top of the type of lead keel that extends well below the wood keel. Unquestionably, the best way to do this would be to drop the lead keel and cover all of the wood, then bolt the lead back through the fiberglass. However, if the keelbolts are sound and tight, you can put off dropping the keel until some future time, rabbet the wood adjacent to the lead, and end the covering against it. Or you can carry the fiberglass onto the lead at least two inches, fasten it with stout screws into both wood and lead, and gain reinforcement to the keel-to-hull join. It hardly seems worth the trouble to rabbet the lead for glass that terminates on it. The stuff is too mean to work. Fairing putty, which sticks well to lead, will blend the covering into the shape quite nicely.

Despite all that is said above, I hope you will decide to cover a wooden centerboard and its trunk. Even if they don't seem to need covering now, it should be obvious that they're bound to need it in time. There is no better time to do it than when the rest of the boat is being covered. Admittedly, centerboards are ruggedly built and it is rarely disastrous to lose one. A well-built wooden case is very durable, too. However, the life of either one can be so greatly extended, maintenance so reduced, and one's peace of mind so reinforced that the covering-and-lining process is well worth doing anytime. Without it, any other covering on the boat must be considered an unfinished job, and the protection of the outside of the hull effectively stops at the garboard plank in way of an uncovered trunk, as well as some distance forward of and abaft of it.

A single consideration controls the covering of these parts — clearance. Obviously, a centerboard must be able to swing freely in the trunk. If it doesn't, you must create clearance. Most of the older wooden trunks with wooden boards were built with generous clearance. It was likely that the lumber in either or both would warp from shrinking, swelling, or aging. Wooden trunks also have a tendency to hourglass, or pinch together in the middle. This is due to the upward and in-

A gouge on a long handle slices away an hourglassed centerboard trunk. (Milton Silvia photo)

ward pressure exerted on them either by the water when afloat or by the blocking on which they rest ashore. A trunk can also get squeezed by the construction through which it passes.

An accompanying photograph shows me with a gouge on a stick shaving out the interior of a Wianno Senior's trunk, which had been severely pinched where the main bulkhead and the cockpit sole converge against its sides. The 1-inch wooden centerboard was jamming in this area of the trunk, which was originally about 1½ inches wide! Coincidentally, the slot in the iron ballast keel of this boat had also been narrowed more than $\frac{1}{8}$ inch by the heavy rust scale accumulated during her many decades of use.

You will have to measure carefully the trunk's internal width and the board's thickness to determine how much clearance is given. Then check the straightness of all your surfaces, since curves and angles can alter the effective clearance. A good way to check out the trunk is to test narrow boards of slightly different widths in it until you find the widest board that will pass through its interior.

Once you know what clearance you have to work with, you can calculate how much fiberglass you can use on the trunk lining and the board and still have some clearance. There should be no less than $\frac{1}{8}$ inch side play in the completed assembly when both are glassed. If the board is wood and not covered, you should allow $\frac{1}{4}$-inch clearance, not for swelling but for warping. In calculating the thickness of the covering and the lining (both of which should be all-matt laminates), you will be safe to count each layer of $1\frac{1}{2}$-ounce matt as $\frac{1}{32}$ inch. It won't come out quite as thick as that unless you are a very sloppy laminator.

The laminate for the trunk and board is best made entirely of matt because the paramount considerations are resistance to wear and imperviousness to water, even when worn part-way through. Further, matt won't peel or delaminate nearly as readily as roving or cloth. This is important on something as likely to be banged as a centerboard, or chewed by stones jammed between board and trunk.

Quite possibly, there will not be enough clearance for both a substantial lining in the trunk and a stout covering on the board, so you'll be looking for more space. Naturally, the trunk doesn't lend itself to easy enlargement (unless you want to tear it apart). It's rough enough just to slice away the hump caused by hourglassing.

A wooden centerboard can be thinned down with a hand electric plane and/or a high-speed grinder with coarse paper. Some boards can even be run through a thickness planer; however, if the planer's knives strike a drift bolt, don't tell the operator I sent you! A second possibility is to make a new board, one thin enough to allow for the laminate both on itself and within the trunk. With its laminate, it will be stronger than a thicker board.

If necessary, you can go from a wooden board to a metal one, unless this is prohibited by class racing rules, as it was with the Wianno Senior mentioned above. Steel is the cheapest metal for a centerboard. If I were to build a board in steel, I would either coat it with zinc-loaded paint or have it galvanized, and then I would cover it with fiberglass. A steel plate ⅛ inch thick with four or five layers of 1½-ounce matt on each side will be stronger than a 1-inch wooden board. Out of the water, the covered steel board will weigh 5 pounds per square foot, just about the same as a similarly covered 1-inch oak board. The steel will weigh almost four pounds per square foot underwater, due to its greater density, while the oak would have approximately neutral buoyancy without its added lead weight. This means a steel board will be hard to raise, and you may need some mechanical advantage to help you with it.

Although it is more expensive, marine aluminum makes a better metal core for such a replacement centerboard because it is less than one-third the weight of steel and because it won't erupt with rust if exposed.

As a rough guide to thickness, we have found over the years that three to four layers seem to be enough on boards up to 1 inch thick, and four to six on boards up to 2 inches. Where the pivot pin and pendant hardware are fitted to a board, all holes through the board should be bored oversize, never less than double the pin size. Fill each hole with chopped glass in resin, many little discs of matt, or body putty; and rebore for the pin or eyebolt. If this is done before the board is covered, so that the filler is within the covering, it will seal out water and provide a noncorrosive bearing area as well.

If the trunk is a physically sound structure, the thickness of its liner should be at least the same as given above for its board, and, depending on its size, it would certainly be good to add some more layers if there is room for them. It is my opinion that a trunk liner should be all matt because it is subjected to much wear, and I don't like the idea that the board might tangle with any roving that might become exposed and possibly peeled out. Anyway, the strength of roving is hardly needed, whereas the liner is well supported on all sides by the existing trunk. Building the liner is not difficult, but you will have to make some careful measurements if you want it to come out just right. Should you make it bigger than the trunk on its outside, or smaller than the board on its inside, you will have to rework it.

A bilgeboard trunk liner for an Atalanta sloop, after its male mold was pulled. The recess in the upper forward corner of the liner accommodates a bearing plate on the inside of the trunk. (Milton Silvia photo)

The best way to fabricate a liner seems to be to lay it up on a male mold. The mold is merely a slab or a box that is easily made of Masonite or plywood to the shape wanted. Around or against the bottom of the mold you will want to build a flange on which to laminate an integral flange at the bottom of the liner. This flange will fit against the bottom of the keel, and the hull covering will overlap it to make a single-piece liner and covering.

The mold will not be removed easily from some liners after layup because of the great depth of the liner. However, the situation will not be too bad if the top of the trunk for which the liner is being made is open or partly open. In that case you will have an opening in the top of the liner through which to drive the mold out of the bottom. Even if the trunk top is closed, however, you can leave one or two openings in the top of the liner for this purpose and patch them after it is out of the mold. In any event, the mold should be waxed very heavily with mold-release wax before the liner is laid up on it. Also, although most centerboard trunks are already designed and built longer on the bottom than at the top, you should make sure that this is true of your mold, and that the top is at least no thicker than the bottom.

When you install the liner in the trunk, you will want to fasten it in place. The most important attachment is a row of mechanical fastenings around the flange up into the keel, before it is joined to the hull covering with an overlap of fiberglass. As for fastenings within the box, I do not consider it wise to put screws into the sides where the rubbing of the centerboard might uncover them, especially along the bottom.

If the trunk is open at the top or has a removable cap, you can lay up along the top of the sides of the liner a fiberglass angle that turns onto the top edge of the trunk sides and is fastened down into the wood, or you can run a row of fastenings around the top of the liner itself. Naturally, the former is the better method, and the trailing edge of the centerboard is usually thin enough to allow plenty of room for an extra thickness of fiberglass at the top of the trunk.

While the liner is being installed, its sides should be kept well wedged against the sides of the box. The most even pressure can be applied with pairs of long wedges made by diagonally splitting boards that are a bit taller than the liner (so that their ends will hang out of the bottom and/or top) and a tiny bit wider than its inside width. When you reassemble the two pieces in the lined trunk and pound on a wide end, the liner will spread uniformly from top to bottom.

For fastening the sides of the liner to the sides of the box, I worked out the following system: Before installing the liner, bore some sizable holes in the sides of the trunk with a hole saw (any size from 1¼ inches to 3 inches), and flare their outboard edges. After the liner is wedged tightly against the trunk, fill the holes with discs of matt and resin, or body putty. These inverted-cone-shaped knobs built onto the liner should lock it solidly to the sides of the trunk.

To make a watertight seal around the centerboard pivot pin, bore out the hole in the keel or centerboard trunk to a much larger diameter, but do not bore the liner. Fill these holes against the liner as described above, then rebore the solid glass plug built for the pin or bolt, all the way through everything. If the pin is a bolt through the trunk, inside the boat, use leather washers under the head and under the nut to seal out water. If the pin is through the keel outside the boat, you can seal the hole by capping it with layers that are part of the hull covering, which will also serve to retain the pin.

Needless to say, if you have an underwater or watertight centerboard pendant attachment, you will have to find a method similar to the above to connect the wire sheave boxes and/or tubing directly to the fiberglass of the liner. It might mean wrapping a tube with fiberglass, or bolting a sheave-box to the top of your liner, but I know you can work it out. Do not leave any avenue for water to enter the wooden construction, lest the whole purpose of the liner be defeated.

COVERING LAPSTRAKE BOATS

A lapstrake hull is bound to take more time to cover than a carvel-planked hull. It takes skill and patience to tuck the fiberglass into the corners of the laps, but we do it all the time, so you can, too. It is not necessary to fill in each lap with a ramp of putty or a strip of triangular molding over which to roll the glass. That trick works all right, and it does make covering easy, but it also spoils the crisp plank lines that are the essence of a lapstrake boat's traditional appeal. Filling in the laps will also, by the way, spoil the tendency of the laps to make the boat drier by deflecting water that slides up her topsides.

It is best not to overdo any softening of the laps, but if you must, put a small bead of putty in the very apex of the lap. Smooth it with your finger or the end of a small dowel that has been sanded blunt. See that it fairs into the underside of the lap about halfway between the inner corner and the outer corner. This way, you will have a better-looking lap that still throws a shadow and deflects spray.

A stronger way to cover a lap is to lay a small string of strand roving into the inner corner. This is done by preparing many short strings, two to three feet long (whichever length you can handle best), which are hung in a row over a stick within reach. Each string is taken in turn, dipped into the resin bucket, drawn between thumb and finger, stretched along the lap, and wiped out straight with the brush. Strand roving goes on best when the strands are dipped by one man, who then helps a second man hold it in place until the second man's brush has secured it in the corner.

Of course it is much easier to cover an upside-down lapstrake boat, but you can't always have it that way. Here, then, is how you can minimize the difficulties of glassing a tipped-down boat:

1. Don't try to cover more than one lap at a time. Cut the matt into strips that are less than two planks wide, leave the top edge as cut, and comb the bottom edge. Fit the top edge against a lap, then smooth the matt down over the first plank, around the lap, and onto the second plank. Fit the next piece into the lap just covered, so that it will cover the second plank, the second lap, and end on the third plank. The second plank now has two layers, and so will the third plank when you fit the next piece into the second lap, and so on.

This process gives you two layers on enough of each plank the first time around to put in your fastenings where they count most. Fasten just under the lap in each plank through two layers, and, with every other fastening staggered lower on the plank, as far as you have two layers. You do not need to put fastenings in the lower edge of each plank, which already has the original lapstrake fasteners in it and may be a bit split anyway. If you were to continue as above, you would always have fewer layers down around the lap than on the surface of the planks. But you can catch up anytime you want by putting on pieces with both top and bottom edges combed on the laps only. Meanwhile, all of the rest of the layers can be butted or blended in the centers of the planks. If the edges of the laps become blunt, a cut edge laid up to them will help.

Whatever system you work out, the importance of covering only one lap at a time will come home to you if you try to cover more than one. Every time you push the matt into one lap, it will pull out of the one above or below it. It's enough to drive you out of your mind, and it's also bound to produce a row of bubbles in the inner corners.

2. Use only matt in covering the laps. It simply isn't

worth the struggle to try to keep roving bent around such tight, S-shaped corners. If you have split planks, opened scarphs, or other local problems, you can apply some strips of roving no wider than the particular plank. But if the weakness involves the laps, it is better to pile on enough layers of matt to restore strength. Incidentally, a laminate with a lapstrake configuration is stiffer and therefore stronger than a smooth laminate because poor resistance to bending is one of the greatest drawbacks of fiberglass.

3. Butt or comb all end joints in the matt and stagger the joints.

4. Don't forget to paint the surface ahead with resin and let it get sticky. This is especially important, since pushing the matt into the laps tends to dislodge it from the surface and encourages it to fall off the boat.

5. When you buy the matt for a lapstrake boat, get a soft matt, one with a minimum of starch in it. Such matt will form laps more easily and it will wet out more quickly.

If you do a good job on a lapstrake boat, you will have something to be proud of, and you can consider yourself qualified to cover any wooden boat. Further, the covering of a lapstrake boat is, more often than with any other kind, the only way to save her from impending doom. If she's a good boat, you will have done a good thing.

Over the years, the system described in this book has developed into a well-proven way to restore soundness and to prolong indefinitely the life of a wooden boat. Comparing its cost with the cost of the never-quite-as-good alternatives, it is a remarkably economical system.

11/   Some Case Histories

As I write this, more and more examples keep coming to mind — boats as short as 10 feet and as long as 65 feet; as light as 70 pounds and as heavy as 70,000 pounds; dainty daysailers and ungainly draggers. I'd like to tell about all of them, but that's because I have a one-track mind and will talk about boats nonstop until there's nobody left to listen.

I have been saying for years that there are thousands of good, old wooden boats deserving of a happy ending: to sail on and on without faltering, to give another span of years of sailing pleasure beyond her normal life expectancy. A good covering job will do it; and what more could any boat, or boat owner, ask?

Reluctantly, but mercifully, I've limited the following case histories to a handful of boats chosen mostly as representative of a type and the problems to be expected with it, so that the methods and laminates can be described. The jobs are roughly in chronological order, and in the order of the learning process involved as we applied and developed the system.

Two guidelines helped me weed out boats pressing to be described: (1) I avoided mention of any boats not well tested. This eliminated all of the boats that we covered within two years except one. (2) I mentioned only one boat of a type or size. This worked well until I got to the "Novis," of which we have done so many that I just couldn't discuss only one.

ED WALSH'S SKIFF

When Ed Walsh closed his general store in Mattapoisett, Massachusetts, and retired, he brought us his heavy, tired, old 16-foot flat-bottomed skiff and asked us if we could make her seaworthy for a reasonable sum. We really couldn't, because she needed drastic rebuilding. But, unwilling to deny this unanimously beloved patriarch his favorite pastime of handlining, I decided to try covering her with many layers of matt, just as though we were building a fiberglass boat. We left the paint on and used galvanized nails to hold the "two boats" together.

I don't remember the schedule, but she probably got at least six layers of 1½-ounce matt on the bottom and four on the topsides. Galvanized shingle nails were used after a couple of layers. I remember the men who were doing this unheard-of job saying, "Mr. Vaitses, this is crazy! Nobody puts more than a layer or two on any boat."

Ed's skiff was the first boat on which we applied enough glass to get along, in effect, without the wood. To see Ed goin' fishin' without problems gave us courage in later years to rebuild bigger and more complex boats with heavy, fastened-on coverings.

THE RAM ISLAND

The *Ram Island* was a 32-foot Novi we built about 15 years ago for Van Clark, and he wanted her covered with fiberglass. He was a customer who was always getting us into something new, and this was the first sizable boat we had ever been asked to cover. I had yet to come up with the idea of mechanical fastenings, but Van and I were both well aware of the danger that the fiberglass might part company with the wood. The system that we developed for her carvel cedar planking was to caulk her seams just a touch higher than the surface with strips of fiberglass matt. Before we covered her, we saturated the matt-filled seams with resin. Our hope was that the covering would be retained by what was, in effect, an attached flange projecting into every seam of the planking.

The *Ram Island* has lived in the water year round, serving as a ferry to the Clarks' island home. A belt of oak sheathing and a bronze bow piece were fitted for ice breaking, and she is kept at her timber-shivering chores each winter until the ice won't give way.

It would seem that the method of making the fiberglass fast to the *Ram Island* worked well enough. I think it had something to do with the cedar planking, which is nowhere near as "pushy" when swelling as some of the harder woods. In any case, it was an obvious leap from this relatively involved procedure to that of fastening a covering with the power staplers we already had in the shop for cold-molding and other wood laminating jobs. Why we didn't think of the staples first, I can't imagine. Perhaps the missing link was driving the staples before the fiberglass got too hard to accept them. Or possibly it had not occurred to us that the staples could be covered with more layers. Whatever the case, fastening the *Ram Island's* covering was the beginning of a good idea. It just took a while to develop a handier method.

ST. PIERRE DORY

This St. Pierre dory was built for use on the Great Lakes with a double-planked, drier-than-usual oak bottom and bolted lapstrake marine plywood side planking on sawn frames. When the oak bottom swelled and buckled so much that it broke the bottom frames, the owner told us to "put the best damned bottom you can think of on her." I opted for a double-planked cedar bottom heavily covered with fiberglass, which, if memory serves, we carried above the load waterline up against the underside of the lap of one of the planks. Worse, it was closely fastened or pinched with a metal strip along its edge. Unfortunately, an overhanging rabbet was not used in the thin plywood planking. In fact, I hadn't yet thought of such a possibility.

The owner was delighted to "sweep out the bilge with a dust pan" thereafter; but years later I got a distress call from the man who bought the boat from the owner's estate. Rot was raging through the plywood side planks just above and below the termination of the covering.

The unexpected, early rot problem in this boat brought home to me the importance of keeping fresh water from getting behind the covering, and it started me thinking about overhanging rabbets. On lakes, where not only rainwater but all of the water is fresh, it wouldn't seem wise to terminate a covering anywhere, or in any way, that water could possibly get behind it. Indeed, for service in "sweet water," I think I would saturate the underlying wood thoroughly with preservative, use epoxy resin next to the wood, and *not* terminate the covering below the deck.

If my experience with this boat chalks one up for the epoxy sheathing boys, so be it. I believe one must face his mistakes; otherwise, he cannot learn and grow. Without the warning of this early failure, I hate to think how many saltwater boats that we subsequently covered might have had rot problems along careless deck or hull terminations.

SCOTER

Scoter was a 42-foot tandem-centerboard, double-cabin cruising ketch designed by the John Alden office to be similar to the then-popular Newporter, but bigger, more sophisticated, and with a round bottom. The Newporter was a V-bottomed production boat with a sheet plywood skin thinly covered with fiberglass. The Alden people thought there might be a market for boats with a plywood-and-glass composite construction.

I worked out the following rather unusual (for that time) construction: Double-diagonal fir-plywood planking covered with at least ⅜ inch fastened-on fiberglass. Decks, houses, and midships cockpit were also fiberglass-covered plywood. Her coamings, trim, and companionway doors were of teak. The keel was laminated of plywood from stem to transom; but the deadwood, which had a fiberglass aft centerboard trunk, a tube for the centerboard pendant, and the shaft log buried in it, was assembled in two halves around these on top of the upside-down hull. This latter plywood structure was built with the sheets running vertical. In the accompanying photograph, you can see the half-built deadwood with its centerboard trunk and shaft log, and some keel bolts with L-ends to anchor them into notches in the plywood. (The centerboard pendant tube is already buried in the plywood.)

A year or two after *Scoter* was built, the Alden people called and asked how I handled the fact that the tube and shaft log conflicted. "I moved the trunk to one side and the shaft log to the other within the skeg," I said, adding defensively, "I didn't think it would affect her performance at all." They agreed.

Scoter's plywood bulkheads were fiberglass-tabbed to the inside of the plywood planking, just as bulkheads are tabbed to fiberglass hulls, with strips of matt and roving, and the tabbing was mechanically fastened to both. Any joints needed in the bulkheads were made by

rabbeting the sheets along the butted edges, ⅛ inch deep at most and about 3 inches wide, and filling these wide, shallow recesses with layers of fiberglass that spanned the butt joint. This was done on both sides of the bulk-heads, fastened mechanically, and sanded flush. The exterior of the cockpit bulkheads and the trunk sides and ends were also covered with fiberglass.

Despite the many odd features of her construction, *Scoter* turned out all right, and no doubt she has required less maintenance than an all-wood boat. However, she was not radically inexpensive to build, even when compared with other custom boat constructions. Perhaps the fiberglass-covered plywood was economical, but putting a yacht finish on her topsides cut deeply into those savings, partly due to the state of the art at that time.

What *Scoter* has proved in the long haul is that composite plywood-and-fiberglass construction can work, that you can tab wood to wood with fiberglass if you use mechanical fastenings, and that a fiberglass-covered wooden boat can look (and be) as chic and expensive as any other.

BLACK WITCH

Black Witch was a 57-foot steel yawl, not exactly appropriate for this book, but interesting nevertheless. She was said to have immigrated to the United States from the Baltic at about the time of World War I. She was rusted until she was so thin that young Jay Coffman, who bought her in the 1960s, put his disc sander through her bottom. When told that covering her with fiberglass might make her float again, he got bids from two fiberglass production companies and my shop. We won the job at $6,000, and, incredibly, made a profit. I don't know what the other bidders had in mind at twice the price, but my scheme was to lay this 45,000-pound monster on one side and then the other, completing the work with each side in a favorable position, and overlapping the laminates from the two sides across the bottom of the keel.

We put on a half-inch of alternate matt and roving, cartridge-fired hardened steel nails with large, tarpaper washers under their heads through both glass and steel, and covered these with another half-inch of glass. We carried the covering over her steel bulwarks and down onto the covering board of the teak deck, which we did not cover. I felt that at least this "hook" of fiberglass over the bulwark would always keep the two "hulls" locked together.

Looking back, it seems that the covering on *Black Witch* was almost ridiculously heavy. She spent three years in the Caribbean and then crossed the Atlantic, losing both masts on the way, but without a trace of hull trouble. No wonder.

I learned two things from *Black Witch*. (1) She had a small leak through a massive two-inch-thick overlap in our covering on the bottom of the keel when launched. Out she came to get a patch and some U-shaped covering on the whole keel. Now you know why I prefer U-shaped layers on any keel first — and more matt, less roving. (Matt is watertight; roving isn't.) (2) When she was back in the water, she only went down halfway to the raised waterline I had carefully calculated for her. I was right that steel soaks up no water, but I had not realized that two-thirds of the underwater fiberglass would be floating itself!

One other special problem with *Black Witch* might be of interest. Between her hull and deck she had an extra-heavy pipe rudder port (or tube) that was in excellent condition. It fitted the rudder stock too closely to accept a fiberglass liner connected to the covering. On the other hand, the bottom plating around its base was not stout enough to be trusted with the bolts of a metal ring clamping the covering to the bottom, if we simply terminated the covering at the edge of the port's exit. I decided to wrap the outside of the tube — inside the boat — with fiberglass, which was extended out as a flange on the inside of the bottom plating a foot or more. The covering on the outside and the flange on the inside were then bolted together with many closely spaced bolts, making a sandwich of the bottom plating. The bolts, of course, were covered with more fiberglass on both the inside and the outside of the boat.

WINDERMERE

Windermere is a neat 34-foot Alden yawl built in 1928. In the late 1960s, John Collamore II reluctantly put her up for sale for $10,000, "because she needed too much work." He hadn't had even an insulting offer in many months when he saw that we were covering boats that were older and in worse shape than his. Since this was just what she needed, John sailed her around to Mattapoisett from Barrington, Rhode Island, to get the treatment. I happened to catch sight of her that Sunday afternoon as she scudded up the harbor in a fresh sou'west breeze. She made a beautiful picture. But Monday afternoon, when the hauler went to pull her out at the town pier, she was deep in the water and flooding fast.

We covered *Windermere* with a generously thick laminate. Her hull got ⅜ inch on the topsides, ½ inch on the bottom, and no doubt more around her iron keel. We literally built a fiberglass hull around her. We also covered her main deck and her cockpit, both of which had been getting a little loose. I don't remember how many laminates were used on those areas, but our habit in those days was to use plenty of glass.

Soon afterward, John and his son, John III, moved to Deltaville, Virginia, where they founded Hulls Unlimited - East Inc. to build fiberglass boats. Since the early 1970s, *Windermere* has lived year round in the tidewaters of the Rappahannock River. Every year, when they haul her out for a week of painting, the Collamores look and poke and thump, but they have yet to find any sign of trouble. *Windermere's* homeport is far enough south for a boat to have plenty of steamy, rot-breeding days, so I have been most interested to know how she is faring as the years go by. Needless to say, the Collamores' consistent reports of "A-1 condition" and "no sign of rot" have been music to my ears.

KATAMA

Katama was a Clinton Crane-designed 54-foot sloop built in 1914 by Hodgdon Brothers in East Boothbay, Maine. She had the spoon bow, shoal hull, and long overhangs of her time, and the deep, short, fin keel that is still popular. Her enormous gaff rig had been replaced with a low-aspect-ratio, seven-eighths Marconi rig, but she was still a "goin' boat" in a breeze. By the time she was nearing 60 years of age, the white lead between her double planking had crumbled, and she was getting very limber. Her owner was my son, Stephen, and each time he sailed her hard, it took longer for her leaks to settle down. When she sank one day at the pier, he was convinced that she should be covered.

When we got around to the job, she was hemmed in, without enough room on either side to lay her over on her sides. Putting the fiberglass up under those overhangs was quite a chore. It had to be done in many small pieces, because I hadn't yet figured out the sticky resin trick. We took two pieces about 18 inches square (in the directly overhead areas), presaturated them with the two edges overhanging each other by about three inches, and put them up with four hands. This produced a pattern in which one layer overlapped the other everywhere by three inches. It went pretty fast with a crew of three: one saturating the squares and two putting them up. But it was antediluvian compared to the sticky resin method, with which two men could have put up 38-inch-by-6-foot pieces much more quickly.

The laminate thicknesses were ⅝ inch on the topsides, 1 inch on the bottom and keel, and 1½ inches across the garboards, down onto that deep fin, and around the leading edge. The deck got six layers tucked into an overhanging rabbet a couple of inches up on the teak trunk sides. I believe this was the first time we cut an overhanging rabbet. (Steve is very fond of brightwork or I'd have made a fiberglass mummy of the boat.)

Katama's toerails and coamings were removed so that the deck laminate joined the hull and was continuous into the cockpit. Her rudder port was lined with a fiberglass tube. All through-hulls were removed and replaced over the covering. Steve spent a month of his own time, with the help of friends, fairing and polishing her hull and spray painting the topsides. His father allowed that this biggest-yet covering job was also the best looking yet; but, more important, for the first time in many years *Katama* was fit to take outdoors.

An outside passage was just what Steve undertook that first fall — from Connecticut to the Bahamas. In the next five or six years she made that round-trip twice and cruised extensively at both ends. She encountered enough gales offshore to lose a shroud, break her main boom, blow out some sails, and have to be hove-to with her crew pretty much confined below for 19 hours on one occasion. Yet, knowing what she had around her, we never feared for *Katama's* survival at sea — at least not until Steve sent her south with a green crew who panicked and lost her against the side of a freighter.

We learned a startling lesson about soakage when we covered *Katama*. She had lived in the water year round for perhaps 20 years before she was brought ashore to await covering. On the way to the yard, she weighed 32,000 pounds soaking wet. After three years ashore, having been covered with the laminate described above, and with 800 additional pounds of replaced engine and generator aboard, she still weighed 32,000 pounds! She was also floating a little higher than her pre-covering waterline. About three years after she was relaunched, she was just about down to her pre-covering waterline. But then she spent a year in the Bahamas, much of it at anchor, and during that time she climbed well above the line again. The lesson? A wooden boat can soak up a *lot* of water.

One time, going through the East River in New York with a fair tide and the engine hooked up, *Katama* was crowded out of the channel by a tow off LaGuardia Airport and hit a rock so squarely on the leading edge of the keel that it stopped her dead. It was a terrific blow. She lost some fiberglass from her covering, and it was not repaired for a year, but she did not leak or seem to have suffered any permanent damage. Fiberglass is pretty good stuff, and when it's backed up all over by a wooden boat, it's terrific.

JIM BLADES' LOBSTER BOAT

One July day when I came back to the shop from lunch, a lobsterman was waiting to see me. He had heard that we put fiberglass on wooden boats. "Sure do," I allowed. Never dreaming what was coming, I asked, "What kind of a boat do you have?"

Jim had taken delivery of a new 45-footer in February. She was a well-built, rugged, V-bottomed craft with 1½-inch mahogany planking on 3-inch-by-5-inch oak frames. In lieu of caulking, she was covered with two layers of fiberglass cloth (unfastened, of course). Now, after less than six months, the cloth was mostly off the starboard side, and she was leaking through the exposed seams.

When I went to study the boat, she was just as Jim described her, but I was unprepared for the shocking sight of a boat that was bare as a newborn babe on one side. In one way, it was fortunate that she had even, closely fitted seams that did not flood her disastrously

as the covering peeled away. In another way, there was big trouble in her future. If all of her tightly fitted mahogany ever got thoroughly saturated, it would certainly walk right off the boat at the chine corner. I'd seen that happen with too tightly fitted planking.

I explained to Jim that I couldn't just "put some fiberglass back on her." There was no way that a couple of layers of fiberglass, even if they were watertight, could survive on such a massive construction that was already beginning to flex its muscles. The dampness of her environment and the water that sooner or later finds its way below on a lobsterboat would surely swell her enough to pop the glass. Nor did I need a crystal ball to predict that the rest of the original cloth would be off her in a matter of weeks.

Being truly afraid that this situation would prove too much for the heaviest of coverings, my first sugges-

128

tion was that all of her seams be routed out and the hull
caulked in the traditional manner. Jim turned that down
out of hand as much too expensive and time-consuming.
He was already financially strapped from buying the
boat; he couldn't afford to lay her up for any length of
time. "She has to keep working," he protested, "as
long as the lobsters are potting."

Here was a thought. If she *could* keep working
without leaking too dangerously, she would be swelled
up considerably in another month or two. If covered in
that condition, she presumably would proceed to become somewhat drier from then on. Since she would
probably never "grow" bigger than that again, the
covering would stay on her indefinitely.

We decided that Jim would keep her going until
early September, unless the leaking became beyond con-
trol, and then bring her in for as quick a job as we could
do: not more than two weeks if all went well. I con-
tacted the builder, with whom I shared mutual respect,
and he needed no urging to contribute to the cost of the
job. That, plus what Jim could stand, allowed us to put

the minimum covering we dared on such a heavy work-boat. Jim brought her in on Saturday so that her surface would be dry enough on Monday. We finished the job the second Friday night, working overtime to restrike the waterline. We had one chuckle when Jim and his sternman ran out of the yard as we prepared to tip her down. We thought it hilarious that these fellows who had risked their hides fishing a naked, leaky hull for several months could not bear to see her laid gently on her beam's end ashore.

It's been five or six years since Jim's boat was recovered, and there's little doubt in my mind that she is past the danger of shedding her covering through normal swelling. She has been living in the water, longlining every winter and lobstering the rest of the year. I still wouldn't like to see her swamped for a couple of months; and I wouldn't have given her *any* hope of staying out of trouble, no matter what the material, if she had been covered over that tightly fitting, dry, 1½-inch mahogany. No, Sir!

DEFIANCE

Defiance is a 40-foot sloop built by Crosby Yacht Building and Storage in Osterville, Massachusetts, in 1927. She is shoal and wide, with a big cabin and bigger cockpit, like an elongated catboat, and as comfortable as an old shoe.

At first she seemed to need refastening, but then it was found that somebody had already added fastenings between the original nails, so that her planking was pretty well perforated at each rib. What was worse, all of her ribs from amidships aft had that strain of "nail sickness" in which water leaking past rusty fastenings runs down the outboard face of the ribs and rot eats out the rib until it is hollow. From the inside of the boat the ribs look fine, and one surveyor was completely fooled by their appearance; they are really only a shell.

Faced with this situation, Bob Cicchetti, her owner, brought her to us to cover. I worked from the following notes:

1. Six layers on the topsides: 1½-ounce matt; 18-ounce roving; ¾-inch galvanized staples; another layer of matt; another layer of roving; the last two layers matt.

2. Eight layers on the bottom.

3. Because the iron keelbolts are suspect and the whole keel wobbly, about 20 layers in the garboard-to-keel corner over a triangular fillet, tapered out onto hull and down onto keel. Use additional flathead stainless screws along garboard and top of keel.

4. Owner says boat lacks lateral plane to go well to windward; wants one foot added to draft of keel before

covering. Install two pieces of 6-inch-by-6-inch oak, one below the other, under the iron ballast keel, faired with profile fore and aft. Attach to boat with vertical steel straps; wood screwed to oak keel above, and to added oak below iron; machine screwed to iron ballast keel.

5. In covering keel, which now slants to starboard, lay boat down on starboard side (to cover port side first) so that weight of boat will straighten the keel. Shrinkage of covering on port side will pull keel to port.

6. Cut overhanging rabbet along top edge of sheer strake *up into* underside of covering board.

7. Remove outside chainplates. Rout wide, shallow depression in planking wider and deeper than these, and line depression with about six layers. Reinstall chainplates with notches cut in edges to lock into glass; use flathead screws. Cover with topside covering and additional layers, until topsides are fair over chainplates.

8. Remove rudder and cover wooden blade with fiberglass. Extend covering right around the rudder stock and build up a connected collar of glass wrapped around the stock just above and just below the blade to keep water from entering along the stock.

9. Remove heavy bronze rudder port that has worked loose in horn timber and Edson steerer platform; wrap port in fiberglass. Enlarge and flare holes in horn timber and platform. Reinstall port with glass casing on; fill flared holes with chopped-strand putty and matt, tying into bottom covering at bottom, and build flange of fiberglass in flared hole in steerer platform at top.

10. Remove outside stuffing box, cover area under flange, and reinstall stuffing box over covering.

11. Remove all through-hulls, bobstay, boomkin stay, and whisker-stay eyeplates, and replace over covering.

12. Fair hull with pigmented talc and resin putty, and restrike waterline and boot top. Owner will smooth and paint.

Bob did smooth and paint *Defiance,* and he got her pretty quickly into rather nice-looking shape from where we left off. He's an architect with the critical eye needed for his trade, so he knew just where to bear down on her with the sander and fill with putty. She has looked good enough to leave her just as she is for three years in succession, with only the bottom paint renewed each spring. But after the next repainting of the topsides, she will look even better. Meanwhile, Bob is delighted to have a stout boat under him again, especially in case he ever forgets that she draws another foot and hits a rock where there wasn't one before.

Incidentally, she does go to windward better now, and Bob says he's not afraid to sock it to her anymore.

THE "NOVIS"

My apologies to Maine designer/builders for applying the name "Novi" to all of the long, narrow, hard-bilged, planked-down keel, single-screw lobster or fishing boats with high bows and low sterns mentioned below. That's the Massachusetts nickname for any such craft built east of there. These able boats have long been popular with Bay State lobstermen, especially north of Cape Cod, where fishing conditions are not very different from those Down East. Many a well-established Massachusetts lobsterman has a favorite builder or local model and will return to that builder or locality when he needs a new boat.

That was the case with Louis Huskins, who lives beside North River in Weymouth, Massachusetts. Louie was in the habit of going back every six to eight years to the same builder for a new boat. He came to us to talk about covering his current 39-foot boat when she was six years old and still in excellent condition, because, "Everything about her is just right, and I hate to make a change. What I'd like to do is hold her just the way she is for a few more years."

Now, I must admit that, much as I advocated it, I rarely was asked to do a covering job to "hold" a boat. Most were intended to bring her back — indeed, often to save her from the graveyard — and *then* hold her. But Louie is not dean of the local lobstermen by chance. He studied our work and got a firm estimate, but before our first conversation he was probably 90 percent certain that covering was the thing to do. While we were covering his boat, as Louie became confident that our system had a potential for more than "a few more years," he had us do additional work calculated to prolong her resistance to wear and tear. I think Louie's boat was a six-layer hull job, at least below the waterline. His decks and cabin trunk would have been three or four layers; and, as I remember it, we put a patch of extra layers on the hauling side where she would normally be sheathed.

While Huskins' boat was being covered, some other lobstermen from his area showed up "to see what he's up to now."

"They all watch Louie," one said to me. "If his boat works out, you'll get more."

That we did. Among the customers was the Ames family, father and sons, with a nice but seriously ill 22-year-old Novi. She had reached the stage where they had had two pumps in her that were going on every five minutes. Then they had hauled her and "fixed some things," but one pump was still going on every 15 minutes.

Money was tight in the mid-1970s, so despite her age and condition, I think *Tubby* got only the "basic four" layers on her topsides and three layers on her cabin trunk. However, I would assume that she got six layers on her bottom, at least in the garboard area. Neither Mr. Ames nor I can remember for sure, but the best thing is that, as he said to me recently, "She hasn't leaked a drop in four years. When I see somebody having trouble with a leaky boat, I tell them, 'Get it fiberglassed!' "

Then there was Doug Sibold, whose ancient, battered, little Novi was so hogged that she ran bow down. Said Doug, "She plows into it something terrible if you speed her up at all."

If you stretched a string fore and aft along the outside of the bottom through the middle of her deadrise, from the main bulkhead to the transom, you could see that her stern had fallen about two inches. I had set out to show Doug how to fill in the hollow in her run when I noticed that jacking up the stands under her stern straightened her out a little. Seeing this, we left her suspended between stands at the transom, with a block under the forefoot for a couple of weeks. Sure enough, her shape returned to what we judged to be "as built." To help hold her shape, we installed a hogging stringer along the inside of her cockpit in an arch from the cockpit sole at the bulkhead, up to the deck, and back down to the cockpit sole at the transom. We bolted it right through planking and all, because the topsides were all adrift. Then we covered everything we could — cockpit, rails, and topsides down around the turn of the bilge — before we laid her over to do the bottom. Again, I think we used three layers of matt in the cockpit, and probably the "basic four" on the rest of her, with more on the garboards and keel.

To a boatbuilder, the delicate condition of some Novis that are kept fishing in all kinds of weather is a tribute to their wonderful lines, which keep the sea so well that they almost lead a charmed life. Almost. But as Gordon Nichols told me, "Coming in one afternoon in a pretty good blow, I could see her sides moving in and out. I said to myself, 'What am I doing out here with a boat in this condition?' "

Gordon fishes a 25 + -year-old Beals Islander out of Swampscott, Massachusetts. I've never seen a motor launch of any kind with a more harmonious shape than this 38-foot Down Easter. If a lovely shape could beguile the cruel sea, this model must have done it. She

had no specific complaint when Gordon decided he was tempting fate. She was just weak all over. Now, with our standard covering on her, she's had three more years "without a creak or groan."

As anyone reading this book can guess, I am not in favor of thin coverings on carvel-planked workboats. I'd always rather put on too much than take a chance with too little. But what with inflation and the fact that fishermen are not well-heeled yachtsmen, I was forced to review the 10 or so years I'd spent putting ample thicknesses on yachts. Just how thin a fastened-on laminate would one dare use with reasonable certainty of success? That's how I came to work out the "basic four" layers. As mentioned in Chapter 3, this full ⅛-inch laminate, well fastened, is as little fiberglass as I would care to put on any carvel-planked boat longer than 20 feet. So far, the four-layer covering has survived up to six years on a lot of boats where more layers simply were not affordable. The "basic four" system has done a much better job for a lot less money than normal repairs, refastening, and recaulking. But the best thing about a good basic covering is that it's relatively simple and inexpensive to repair it or to add more layers as needed. A covering should be able to last forever, until little is left of the wood inside. Personally, I would be mighty pleased if some good fiberglass coverings kept a lot of the older Novis going for a long, long time. They're a great breed of boats.

LADY ALBERTA

There are literally thousands of wooden, twin-screw, stock motor yachts in service along the East Coast. Their gleaming topsides, posh accommodations, fine engines, and expensive "extras" often disguise a hull that is getting dangerously weary. A few years ago, Arthur McLean, owner of a local boatyard, picked up just such a 43-foot Pacemaker at a bargain price. She was in beautiful condition above the waterline, diesel-powered, and, as the ads say, "loaded." He could have had his men rebuild her bottom as a winter project, and he might have done so if he had not been well aware of our ability to cover her for less than his cost. We put six layers on the bottom — they end in an overhanging rabbet in her boot top for three-fourths of her length forward of the transom. For the rest of the way to the bow, the termination is in the center of a certain plank that rises to perhaps 30 inches above the waterline at the stem. Along the boot top, where the termination of the covering crosses plank seams, the seams are stopwatered with pine dowels under its edge. Her spray rails were left on and covered in place.

Lady Alberta's plank-on-edge keel was quite wobbly, as are so many keels on stock boats. Therefore, before we dared tip her to cover her, we gave her an extra buildup over a fillet in the garboard-to-keel corner of six layers. This was fastened on with #14, stainless steel, flathead wood screws every six inches into the garboard and into the keel, in addition to the usual staples.

Arthur had told me that when *Lady Alberta* was running in heavy weather, he could see the joinerwork moving and watch the plank seams open and close as the seas flexed her bottom. When she was hanging in the Travelift, her joinerwork was distorted so much that the doors and drawers stuck fast in their openings.

To cure the latter defect, we built up belts in the covering of six extra layers from waterline to waterline where the straps of the lift are positioned. Coincidentally, one of these belts was also in way of the engines, which won't do her a bit of harm. To avoid noticeable unfairness, and to spread the strain, the width of each successive layer was drastically increased (probably about two inches on each edge).

Lady Alberta was covered only a year ago, so she breaks the rule I made for myself to tell only about well-

tested boats in this chapter. However, she had the classic problems of her type, for which I wanted to describe some applicable solutions.

Here is a one-season assessment: When Arthur next had her in the slings of the lift, he was delighted to find that all the doors and drawers worked smoothly. He also told me that last summer he ran her in weather he wouldn't have confronted before she was covered, that she was stiff and solid-feeling through it, and that (of course) her bilge was dry at all times. If she can go along like that indefinitely, we will be able to say her covering was a good job.

20 YEARS LATER — AND STILL GOING STRONG

It's been nearly 10 years since I sat down and wrote of the boats — big and small, dainty and ungainly — that helped us fine-tune the process of mechanically fastening fiberglass to wood. In 1981 I chose for case histories boats that represented steps in the learning process, ones that presented certain problems and eventually yielded new options: Hurdles cleared, solutions refined. Back then I wrote of a dozen or so boats from the many we had covered and put back to work, and work they did. I picked boats that had weathered the storm and proved that the process was efficient and effective. When I wrote about those boats in 1981, new fiberglass hulls had afforded some of them another 10 years afloat.

Now, close to a decade has passed by. And we know through tracking down some of our old friends — and through the work of my son-in-law Peter Elen, whose Elen Boat Works in Mattapoisett has carried on the mechanical fastening torch — that we've added 20 to 25 years onto the lives of the many boats we've covered.

We've found four of the boats that served as case studies in 1981. Time, changing ownership, and disconnected correspondence have left the futures of some of the other boats a matter of conjecture. But if these four are any indication, there haven't been too many problems.

The Ram Island

The 32-foot Novi we built in the mid-1960s for Van Clark is still doing fine and is still serving as a year round ferry to Ram Island.

The *Ram Island*'s fiberglass covering has held well, family members report. Her winter ferry duties did prompt one minor patching job — a spot on her bottom that had been pelted by chunks of ice caroming off her propeller. The keelson on the inside had to be replaced recently because of rot brought on by fresh water in the bilge. Since we last wrote about her, the *Ram Island* has also received a new engine, which required reboring the shaft log; and this time, a fiberglass tube shaft log was installed and connected with the fiberglass covering on the outside.

One should bear in mind that a wooden boat covered with fiberglass is not likely to leak any salt water, and certainly not enough to inhibit rot on the interior, which salt water tends to do because it is a mild antiseptic. Some thoughts, then, on any wooden boat that doesn't leak through the bottom: It's most important to prevent fresh water from leaking into the bilge, and equally important to douse the bilge well with preservative about once a decade.

Further, leaks or no leaks, always make sure that all enclosed areas on a wooden boat get a constant circulation of fresh air. Good ventilation goes a long way in heading off rot.

Windermere

Windermere, the 34-foot Alden yawl we covered in the late 1960s, is still living year round in the tidewaters of Virginia's Rappahannock River. A few blisters were found and filled this past winter when she was hauled for work on her masts. Those blisters are not too surprising, really. *Windermere* is approaching 20 years of living in warm, somewhat brackish waters since she was covered. John Collamore told me after the last haul that he wasn't sure whether the blisters might be the osmotic "boat pox." But even if she were to come down with a case of that specifically fiberglass ailment and her bottom had to have a protective coating applied, it would be no big deal. What would this amount to compared with all of the yearly maintenance a 60-year-old wooden boat would need? She was 40 years old and sinking when she came to us, and with her fiberglass hull, she's got a lot of years left.

Lady Alberta

Lady Alberta, the 43-foot Pacemaker with the weary and wobbly keel that Arthur McLean picked up for a steal, did all right for herself after our covering job. She was sold to a skipper who took her from Mattapoisett down to Florida and then out on an extended cruise of the Caribbean. After her southern sojourn she headed back up to the Chesapeake, where she was still living when last heard from. Not bad for a boat that sparked no little worry in Arthur just for a trip across Buzzard's Bay before she was covered.

Shirley Ann

Jim Blades' 45-foot lobsterboat, the benefactor of the quick, minimum coverage job needed to get Jim back out on the water, is still going strong. She's still at it, and working hard longlining out of Sakonnet in the hands of current owner Alan Wheeler.

OTHERS WE'VE HELPED ALONG THE WAY

As the mechanical fastening gospel spread, and I put down my rollers and gelcoat to pursue other interests, my son-in-law Peter carried on the work. His experience over the years at Peter Elen's Boat Works in Mattapoisett and the increasing interest in fiberglassing wooden boats indicate to us that the mechanical fastening process continues to produce results.

Stella G.

What a difference. When Mark Godfried of Magnolia, Massachusetts brought his 50-foot Western-rigged stern trawler *Stella G.* to Elen Boat Works in 1988, she had seen better days. After the covering, a new hull and a new life.

Mehitabel

Mehitabel, a lovely Sam Crocker–designed cruising sloop, came to Elen Boat Works with a stripped out interior: Her owner had been considering a rebuilding

job using only wood. At the Boat Works she got the four basic layers of matt and roving, plus four more around the keel and onto the deadrise. That was five or six years ago, and after rebuilding her interior, her owner's been happy ever since.

Nelo II

Nelo II is a 42-foot Novi owned by Neil Reiss, who has no qualms about taking her lobstering as far as 30 miles offshore. He brought her to Elen Boat Works because he estimated that a new boat of the same size and type would cost between $125,000 and $150,000. Fiberglassing everything: hull, deck, trunk, plus five new fiberglass hatches and new electronics cost less than $40,000. Not a bad deal.

Brooke Leigh Anne

Vibration had brought on some leaking problems for *Brooke Leigh Anne,* a 50-foot gillnetter out of Scituate, Massachusetts, and it was time for a new hull. Peter and his crew used about 50,000 ¾-inch to 1½-inch 16-gauge galvanized staples for the entire project, which started with the basic two layers of matt and roving. After the fastening of those two layers, the keel area was topped off with two more layers of 1.5-ounce matt. The sides and stern were then glassed with another layer of 1.5-ounce matt and one layer of roving, which was also stapled. Everything was topped off with two more layers of 1.5-ounce matt. *Brooke Leigh Anne,* with an all-cypress bottom, had absorbed a good amount of water that its captain estimated was equal to the weight of the glass. The added strength of the glass, he figured, was a favorable tradeoff.

Mill Point

The *Mill Point,* a hard-chine 48-footer, was built in Georgia in 1956 as a sounds shrimper and was serving her owner well in 1986 as a dragger working Vineyard

Sound. But while she was showing a reluctance to reveal her age, owner and skipper Mike DeConinck opted for the fiberglassing to head off the problems that were sure to creep in with each new season.

Mill Point was covered with a layer of 1.5-ounce matt, followed by biaxial roving and another layer of 1.5-ounce matt. Workers used more than 25,000 one-inch galvanized staples set three inches apart. Peter left a 6-inch by ½-inch steel shoe on the keel to give it some hefty grounding protection, and then proceeded to add eight layers of matt from each garboard, overlapping at the bottom of the shoe. Mill Point ended up with 16 layers — about an inch — on the bottom of her shoe. From the garboard to just above the chine, Peter and his crew went with four layers of matt; coming down from the bulwarks to just below the chine they put on another four. This overlapping left the chine with more than eight layers of added protection — an extra ½ inch. Where there was no overlapping the *Mill Point* received about ¼ inch more protection. She was faired and then rolled with four coats of colored gelcoat.

Skipper DeConinck had enough confidence in the added strength of the fiberglass that he didn't even bother to put any extra protection or sheathing in the high impact area where the heavy steel trawl doors come up against the stern quarter. He also found that he could move a good half knot faster.

St. Joseph

The *St. Joseph,* a Scituate party fishing boat, won the often difficult-to-get Coast Guard approval for her new look. Owner Anthony Amato came to Peter looking to cut down on costly maintenance. Because she carried

passengers, every step of the covering process was done under the watchful eye of a Coast Guard inspector. She had no problem in getting her license.

Lorraine L.

Charles Lycette of Magnolia, Massachusetts, a lobsterman since 1933, took *Lorraine L.* to Elen Boat Works in 1984 for the complete works: hull, deck, and wheelhouse. He'd owned the *Lorraine L.* since she was built in Maine in 1948 and was partial to her lines and handling. But she had developed a leak around her shaft log that was proving troublesome. Since the glassing there's been no problem, and she's been virtually maintenance-free. Before the glassing, the skipper would have to wait three or four days just to let her dry out enough for painting. Now he can haul, copper paint the bottom, clean and wax the gelcoat, and have her back in the water within 24 hours.

Appendix

BUYING YOUR RESIN AND FIBERGLASS MATERIALS

You should not even consider covering a boat with fiberglass materials[1] bought at retail prices. Their cost will be from two to three times wholesale prices. What is worse, with all due respect to retailers who stock them, these materials, usually sold in gallon cans, are suitable only for small repair jobs. For instance, the resin is sometimes a thickened (thixotropic) formulation that is designed to stay put in that use, so wetting out large areas with it would be unnecessarily difficult. You should locate the wholesalers, the suppliers of resin in drums and fiberglass in rolls, nearest to you, and order your supplies from them. Fortunately, the fiberglass boat business uses so many millions of gallons of polyester boat resin that there are many large companies

---

[1] I am using "Fiberglass Materials" in the more precise meaning of glass-fiber materials only, not in the other common usage, which is really "fiberglass-reinforced plastics" (FRP), shortened to "fiberglass." (You can't blame people for not always saying, "fiberglass-reinforced plastic boats.")

— such as American Cyanamid, Ashland Oil, Koppers, Marco, and Reichold — not to mention innumerable smaller companies, marketing General-Purpose Boat Resin wherever boats are built or repaired around the world. The competition is stiff, which keeps wholesale prices down.

Now, since most fiberglass wholesalers are set up to supply only manufacturers, boat-repair yards, or other volume users, they might pose one or two small problems for you if you don't happen to own or work in a business through which you can order the materials. So, below is my advice for solving these problems.

• Wholesalers are often protective of their customers' "right" to a lower price, so sometimes they won't sell to the "public" at the same price. This game of monopoly is probably as unconstitutional as any other kind of discrimination, but it's a fact of business life. Therefore, you should dub your covering operation "Bob's Boat Covering," "Wood Fiberglassers," or something like that. Get a rubber stamp or some stationery with that as a heading; open a checking account with the same name if you want; and *always* preface your calls with: "This is Bob Wood of ----- Co."

If the order-taker asks questions, you just add, "We have a new system for covering a wooden boat with fiberglass down here, and we need . . . ."

When the subject of credit arises, as it surely will, say: "We haven't bought any materials from you before, but rather than hold up the order for a credit check, we'll be glad to send a check if you'll call us back with the total. Then you can ship the order right away."

Don't offer to pay C.O.D. unless the company delivers on its own truck or you are "picking up" with your truck. Instead, send a check ahead by mail and offer to pay the freight collect: common carriers don't charge to collect the freight fee, but they charge a hefty fee for collecting the cost of the goods for the supplier. Also, because they are responsible for the collection, truckers always insist on cash or a cashier's check, which is a nuisance if your shipment arrives unannounced in your absence, or when the bank is closed.

• The other little wholesale roadblock you might run into is a state sales tax if your state has one and handles it like my state does. In Massachusetts, only retail sales are taxed, and each manufacturer, middleman, and retailer has a number assigned by the state. He gives the number to his suppliers and does not pay any sales tax unless or until he collects some from the retail customer.

Some wholesalers will accept payment of the sales tax from customers who don't have a number ("yet"), but others simply do not set up the bookkeeping to pay sales taxes, so they must have a number to cover themselves, or else they can't sell. This is where your friend with a company comes in. You can use his number and pay him the sales tax, which is all perfectly legal.

I really don't think you'll have any trouble buying wholesale. It's worth going to some trouble because it means saving sums of money ranging from a few hundred to well over a thousand dollars. You must also remember that wholesalers are in business to sell goods, and that as long as they can't be accused by their retailers of cutting them out, they want your business.

Should you be looking only for enough materials to cover a small boat, however, you will find that there are over-the-counter and mail-order marine discount houses from whom you can buy at considerably less than retail price.

Another source of small quantities is local

fiberglass boatbuilders and repairers. The small- and medium-size companies that are using those materials are often willing to sell you some, or to order some for you on a cash-and-carry basis, at a modest markup of 150 percent to 200 percent of their cost, plus sales tax. I ought to know about that, since I sold tons of the stuff in the 20 or so years that the company I ran had those materials in stock.

WHAT RESIN TO BUY

The best resin for covering wooden boats with fiber-glass, especially on a big job with a small crew, is a low-wax or no-wax type. Without wax, new layers added to layers that have been curing for some days will still bond well with an unsanded surface. A fairly safe rule is that if the surface gums up sandpaper, then it doesn't need sanding to bond well. I have seen some resins stay gummy or "tacky" for weeks.

Except for the need to sand it if left for more than a day or two before "hooking on," any general-purpose boat resin with wax in it will work just as well as low-wax or no-wax resin. You should use the same rule, applied conversely, for resin with little or no wax in it: When it no longer gums up sandpaper, when it is glassy-hard and not at all tacky, you *must* sand it before adding new layers.

HOW MUCH RESIN TO ORDER

In Chapter 2, when I discussed the weight of a covering job, I said that a square foot of fiberglass laminate ⅛ inch thick weighs one pound. Using this basic fact, you can make a reasonable estimate of the quantity of resin and of fiberglass materials needed for the laminate you plan to put on your boat. Both the books and my experience vary somewhat in estimates of the thickness of the laminates resulting from specific numbers of layers of matt and roving, and of the different weights of these. I have found that if you count every two layers (whether 1½-ounce matt or 18-ounce woven roving) as $\frac{1}{16}$ inch, or as ½ pound per square foot when laminated, then you will be close enough for the purposes of ordering resin (despite the fact that layers often build thickness somewhat faster).

In practice, again, you will use resin at the rate of about 60 percent of the weight of the laminate you are laying up. However, it makes a lot of difference whether your work is resin-rich or resin-starved, how much you waste, and all that. Therefore, in estimating the quantity of resin to buy (the first time, anyway), take 60 percent of the total number of pounds (square feet $\frac{1}{8}$ inch thick) that you plan to lay up and order that many pounds of resin.

For instance, suppose you are going to put on 600 square feet $\frac{1}{8}$ inch thick, or 600 pounds of laminate. This could be a 600-square-foot boat with ¼ inch all over it, or a 400-square-foot boat with $\frac{1}{8}$ inch on the top half of it and ¼ inch on the bottom half. In any case, 60 percent of 600 pounds is 360 pounds, so you need approximately 360 pounds of resin.

Resin is sold in gallon cans, five-gallon pails, and 55-gallon drums. The larger the container, the greater the decrease in the price per pound. One-gallon cans sold by retailers cost more than three times the price of each gallon in a drum sold at wholesale, but the wholesale one- and five-gallon quantities cost much more than the resin in 55-gallon drums.

Since a gallon of resin weighs 10 pounds, the 360 pounds in the example above would be 36 gallons, so you might as well buy a 55-gallon drum (550 pounds).

You will find that it pays to order a little extra rather than to try to get just the right amount. If you fall short, a small additional quantity will cost much more per pound than the original order did. Conversely, any materials left over need not go to waste. If you don't find a use for them for mixing putty, putting on a glaze coat, or other jobs around the boat or house, you'll find them readily resellable to other boat owners, especially fiberglass boat owners. In fact, it's just about impossible to show up along a waterfront with fiberglass materials without someone wanting to know whether he can buy enough of them to do some job on his boat.

HOW MUCH CATALYST TO ORDER

The old rule around the boat shops was always "one gallon of catalyst to a barrel of resin." That allowed just under 2 percent, which was as good a guess as any. In hot weather or well-heated shop conditions, one would certainly use much less; in damp, chilly, or cold conditions, much more. Various resins are catalyzed in various weather conditions all the way from ½ percent to 5 percent. But here, again, a gallon jug of catalyst, 50 percent MEK (or methyl ethyl ketone peroxide), costs far less per pound than any smaller quantities (and a case of four jugs costs less than that). Therefore, you would certainly want to start off with a gallon for a 600-pound job. If conditions are against you, you will be looking for more.

HOW MUCH MATT AND ROVING TO ORDER

At last we have come to some materials that you can measure as precisely as you wish. Measure the boat and tote up the square footage of matt and roving needed to make up the layers you plan to put on the boat, allowing no more than 10 percent extra for torn edges or for scraps. Unless you change your plan, there is little likelihood that you will use a significantly different quantity.

In the above example, if you plan to cover 600 square feet of boat with the basic four layers, you would need 1800 square feet of matt (three layers at 600 square feet) and 600 square feet of roving (one layer), plus about 180 feet of matt and 60 feet of roving for waste.

HOW TO ORDER MATT AND ROVING

It would be easy if you could order your matt and roving by the square footage needed, but, unfortunately, these materials are sold in rolls, and you are charged by the number of pounds in the particular roll — so many cents per pound. Nor is there any industry-wide standard roll size. Rather, up to this time, various manufacturers of matt and roving make up the different weights and kinds of material into rolls of an approximate weight, and each roll is ticketed with the exact weight.

One choice in ordering, then, is to tell the wholesaler's order-taker how many square feet you need, and let him figure out how many rolls you need of the size that he carries. Then he will be able to tell you the approximate weight and price — but not the exact price until the specific rolls are set aside to ship to you.

Your second option is to figure out the weight you need, which will put you and the wholesaler closer to an understanding. The weight of the matt is its weight *per square foot:* 1½-ounce matt weighs 1½ ounces per square foot. So you multiply the footage of matt by 1½ ounces, then divide by 16 (the number of ounces in a pound) to get the number of pounds to order. (Eighteen hundred square feet of matt weighs 2,700 ounces, which, divided by 16, would be 167 pounds. Or, with the 10 percent for waste, it would total 184 pounds.)

The weight of woven roving (as well as of cloth) refers to the weight *per square yard (18-ounce roving weighs 18 ounces per square yard).* Therefore, you have to divide the square footage you need by 9 (the number of square feet in a square yard) to get the number of square yards, multiply that by 18 (ounces), then divide the total ounces by 16 to get the number of pounds to order. (Six hundred square feet divided by 9 equals 66.6 yards, which, multiplied by 18 ounces per yard, equals 1198.8 ounces, which, divided by 16 ounces per pound, equals 74.8 pounds. Or, with 10 percent added for waste, it would total 82 pounds.)

Here, once more, the per-roll wholesale price is so much lower than retail that you can well afford any reasonable extra amount you have to buy in whole rolls.

HOW TO BUY ACETONE

Acetone is the fiberglasser's faithful companion. Without it, catalyzed resin is ruinous to everything it contacts. Fortunately, acetone is a widely used solvent: the first place to look for it is under solvents and solvent reclaimers in the Yellow Pages. The next sources are the manufacturers or the wholesalers of paints and varnishes. The last place is on the retailer's paint or hardware shelf, where the price of a gallon can is shocking.

Reclaimed acetone (sometimes called "stripper") is cheaper than new acetone, but some of that leaves your hands a bit oily or tacky. It could be a bit irritating to people with sensitive skin.

Your working habits will determine the rate at which you use up acetone. Experienced workers, who don't load the tool-storage bucket and the hand-washing can with resin, can get along with no more than five gallons of acetone per drum of resin used. But many short sessions exhaust more acetone per pound of laminate laid up than full working days, so if you are a spare-time fiberglasser, your stop-and-go schedule is bound to be acetone-intensive. Keep it covered, and you will save a lot that would evaporate.

New acetone is reasonably kind to most people's

hands. It lets you know about it if you have a cut, but it is an excellent antiseptic. However, it is extremely volatile. Keep it in a metal container at all times, and remember: *KEEP ACETONE AWAY FROM ALL FLAMES, SPARKS, STOVES, AND HEATERS. NO SMOKING NEAR IT!*

SAFETY TIPS

Fiberglass repair tools and materials are capable of great things, but they are also hazardous. Be circumspect. Treat them with the care they deserve.

• When grinding fiberglass, wear goggles and a toxic-dust mask, if not a respirator. Direct the debris stream away from you.

• When grinding or laminating, consider using disposable Tyvek suits. These can be difficult to find, but disposable clothing is usually no farther away than a Salvation Army or Goodwill store, or the back of your closet.

• Wear disposable gloves at all times. Gloves don't get dermatitis. Use drip guards (such as half of a hollow rubber ball) on tools. Barrier creams provide an extra layer of protection.

• Styrene, which comprises 40 percent of polyester resin by weight, is a strong skin and mucous membrane irritant and has exhibited long-term neurotoxicity among fiberglass workers, leading to premature senility. Compared with epoxies, polyester resins are relatively benign, but don't take chances. Wear a respirator when laminating.

• Acetone, the solvent most commonly used by fiberglass workers to clean hands and tools, causes dermatitis and, in large quantities, causes central nervous system dysfunction. In addition, the vapors are explosive. Do not smoke; tolerate no open flames; do not use electric tools around acetone.

- Catalysts, such as MEKP, can splash when poured. Keep them away from your eyes, preferably with goggles. If you're unsuccessful, flush eyes immediately with cold water.
- Accelerators have no place in an amateur boatshop. Buy a resin with the correct formulation, and adjust cure times with catalyst.
- Although epoxy smells less formidable than polyester resin, it is actually more toxic, causing skin irritation, headaches, and nausea. In addition, the effects are cumulative. The more you use it, the worse the effect.
- Keep fire extinguishers handy; use big fans to ventilate; closely follow manufacturers' safety recommendations.

NEW MATERIALS FOR CLEANUP

Until recently, acetone, lacquer thinner, and other solvents, but particularly acetone, have been the accepted agents for removing resin from hands and tools. But they have problems: They can contribute to severe dermatitis; because the dissolved resins are held in solution, they present hazardous waste disposal problems; and they are extremely flammable. More than 3,000 boatshop fires have been directly attributed to acetone.

Now there are alternatives to acetone: emulsifying cleaners that can do the job without visiting harm on the user or the environment. There are perhaps as many as 12 such cleaners now available. One of the first emulsifying cleaners, Res-Away, marketed by Norac Co., Inc. of Azusa, California, replaced acetone at boat manufacturers such as Bayliner, Boston Whaler, and Thunderbird.

Emulsifying cleaners are nonflammable, nontoxic, detergents mixed in water and approved by the EPA as nonhazardous. They effectively remove resin from tools and hands, allowing the residue to be polymerized and discarded as solid waste.

Res-Away and other such products aren't quite as effective or fast as acetone; they work better when warm. But the reduced insult to health and the environment and the elimination of the fire hazard make this an efficiency trade-off worth pursuing.

The latest arrival on a rapidly changing scene is DBE, a new solvent developed by DuPont that is both nontoxic and nonflammable and considered to be more effective than emulsifying cleaners. DBE is available from FRP Supply of Teterboro, New Jersey, a DuPont distributor.

More information on materials for cleanup is available from:

Fiberglass Fabricators Association
3299 K Street
Washington, D.C. 20007
Telephone (202) 337-3322

BUYING BRUSHES, ROLLERS, AND PAPER POTS

These items are used so much by painters that they are carried by every paint store, and they are relatively inexpensive. Anyway, your needs are not going to be great enough to warrant much shopping around. If you wash them out faithfully, two to four brushes, two roller handles, a dozen roller sleeves, and two dozen paper pots (sometimes called tubs) will last through the covering of a 50- to 60-foot boat, decks and all. A word of caution: One reason for buying these items from someone who regularly supplies fiberglassers is that you know that their products won't dissolve in acetone or resin.

The best brushes for fiberglassing seem to be white-bristle, plain-wooden-handle, metal-ferrule, "throwaway" brushes.

You should get plain paper pots, not those with a wax film on them. The 2½-quart size is handiest.

Avoid roller handles with a type of plastic in the handles and spool ends that is not solvent-proof. When I have a choice, I'll always take an unpainted wooden handle.

The roller sleeves I like best are the type that are textured or nubbly, and fairly hard.

Many people used grooved aluminum rollers, which need no sleeve, so they must be all right. However, I never felt that they spread the resin around as well in hand-layup work.

BUYING FAIRING COMPOUNDS AND PUTTY INGREDIENTS

Many resin wholesalers also stock polyester-based fairing putties (sometimes called "hull putty"), and some also carry various fillers with which you can make your own. If you want to use talc to make your own, buy it from paint manufacturers or their suppliers; it is relatively cheap.

You can also buy some good fairing putties at auto-parts stores. Just make sure they are polyester-based, and ask which is easiest to sand if you are using it to get a fine finish. It would pay to get some small quantities or samples and try them on the boat before buying a large quantity of one that might make hard work of the finishing. Mor-Bond is a good soft-sanding resin product.

BUYING MARINE PAINT AND GELCOAT

Gelcoat will be carried by your resin supplier. It's thick stuff, and a gallon will cover only 100 to 150 square feet. But that also depends on how you're applying it.

As for paint systems, the best to use on your top-sides are marine paint systems sold by marine suppliers: boat paints are best for boats. You should be careful that you use a primer and finish coat that are recommended for use on fiberglass and are compatible with each other.

WHERE TO GET BOAT-TURNING AND BOAT-LIFTING EQUIPMENT

You can rent hydraulic jacks at tool-rental services, which are listed in the Yellow Pages. Failing that, you might be able to rent one from a local boatyard or house-mover.

Brownell boat stands also might be rented from a boatyard that uses them. If you are near enough to rent stands from Brownell Boat Works, or want to inquire as to who has them near you, the address is: Brownell Boat Works, 1 Park Street, Mattapoisett, Massachusetts 02739 (telephone: 617-758-2413).

Don't forget that you can also hire a crane to lower your boat on each side. The capacity of the crane, at the boom angle used, should be at least 75 percent of the boat's displacement; the boom's hoisting block should be positioned directly above where the rail of the boat will be in its lowered position. The strap (or straps — two spread fore and aft are better than one) should pass under the hull to the other side of the keel. There it can be fastened to a block that cannot be pulled through under the keel. Or it can be tied off up around the hull to a strong place on deck. It is important that the pull be fairly straight upward from the lowered rail, because too much angle toward or away from the boat will tend to drag it off the keel blocks either toward or away from the crane. But a good operator or "rigger" should have a feel for the operation: that's his business.

WHERE TO GET STAPLERS AND STAPLES

Some sources for renting (or borrowing) staplers are mentioned in Chapter 7, but you can find the manufacturers and/or their representatives listed in the Yellow Pages.

Don't forget that if you can't get heavy staples, power-driven, many other fastenings will work. There's nothing wrong with the lowly galvanized asphalt shingle nail, and you can buy them, in any length, just about anywhere. Just make sure you put plenty of fastenings in your covering.

Index